THE FORM
OF THE BOOK

ESSAYS ON THE MORALITY
OF GOOD DESIGN

Jan Tschichold

TRANSLATED FROM THE
GERMAN BY HAJO HADELER
EDITED, WITH AN INTRODUCTION,
BY ROBERT BRINGHURST

Hartley & Marks
PUBLISHERS INC.
1991

Published by
Hartley & Marks Publishers Inc.
P.O. Box 147, Point Roberts
Washington 98281

3661 West Broadway
Vancouver, B.C.
V6R 2B8

Originally published in German as
*Ausgewählte Aufsätze über Fragen der
Gestalt des Buches und der Typographie*
by Birkhäuser Verlag, Basel, © 1975
Translation Copyright © 1991 by
Hartley & Marks, Inc. Intro-
duction Copyright © 1991
by Robert Bringhurst

ISBN 0-88179-116-4

Printed in the U.S.A.

If not available at your local bookstore,
this book may be ordered directly from the publisher.
Send the cover price plus one dollar fifty for
shipping costs to the above address.

LIBRARY OF CONGRESS CIP DATA

Tshichold, Jan, 1902-1974
[*Ausgewählte Aufsätze über Fragen der
Gestalt des Buches und der Typographie.* English]
The form of the book : selected essays on questions of book
design & typography / Jan Tschichold ; translated from the German by Hajo
Hadeler ; edited, with an introduction, by Robert Bringhurst.
p. cm.
Translation of: *Ausgewählte Aufsätze über Fragen der
Gestalt des Buches und der Typographie.*
Includes index.
ISBN 0-88179-116-4 (pb : acid-free)
1. Book Design. 2. Printing, Practical--Layout. I. Title.
Z116.A3T7613 1991 91-33828
686--dc20 CIP

Table of Contents

Introduction

TYPOGRAPHY, in the Newtonian view, is nothing very interesting or mysterious; it is simply mechanized writing. Now that the silicon chip has joined the wheel, the lever and the inclined plane, typography is also computerized, digitized writing: more complex than it was, but no more profound, and perhaps increasingly subject to fashion.

Seen with fresher eyes, or from a warier perspective, typography still evokes the wonder and fear with which it startled the medieval world. It is a black art that borders on artificial insemination, and it can pose equally difficult moral questions. Type is writing that is edited, shaped, doctored, and made to reproduce itself through artificial means; and writing itself is a kind of gene-bank for ideas. Confined within the schools, typography is a means of implanting the fruits of chosen minds and lives into the minds and lives of others. Set loose in the world, it is an uncontrollable vector, like the malaria-bearing mosquito, able to spread ideas as indiscriminately as viruses or germs. The possibilities for its use and abuse are potent and legion.

Like other arts, from medicine to music, typography also demands both close proximity and distance. This is not what it sounds like, a schizophrenic sense of scale, but a kind of taut completeness. Typography is a process, after all, in which large objects – epics, encyclopedias and bibles, for example – are built from minute components, such as the strokes and bowls of letters. It is work, therefore, in which macroscopic and microscopic perspectives constantly converge. As if that were not enough, it's also an enterprise in which history is continuously present, and must therefore be kept continuously alive. These are among the things that make it unmechanical and nourishing.

Jan Tschichold was a lifelong student, teacher and practitioner of typography, passionately concerned with the broadest principles and tiniest details of his chosen art and craft. He was also an artist preternaturally conscious of the history of his profession and the materials he handled day by day. What he thought about and worked with on a daily basis was, to him, not merely metal, ink and paper but the history of literature, of letterforms, and of the book as a cultural force for conservation and for change.

Tschichold was born in Leipzig in 1902. In his early years, he studied painting and drawing in that city full of memories of Leibniz, Goethe, Luther, Bach and Mendelssohn. There is a story that, at 12 years old, the would-be artist grew so dissatisfied with the appearance of a novel he was reading that he redesigned its title page and vainly tried to alter the flow of the text. Six years later, still in his native city, he was teaching as well as studying graphic design and typography.

In 1925 he moved briefly to Berlin, and in 1926 to Munich. In 1933, after six weeks' imprisonment for practising an aesthetic of which the National Socialist Party disapproved, he escaped with his wife and infant son to Switzerland. Thus began an exile that never came to an end. He made occasional brief visits to France, Scandinavia, Britain and the USA, and he spent two years with Penguin Books in London; that apart, Tschichold lived and worked in Switzerland from 1933 until his death at Locarno in 1974.

Like every conscious artist, he looked intently and analytically at whatever he admired. He measured early books and manuscripts, recorded dimensions, sketched page shapes and letterforms. The most important result of this lifelong habit, apart from his own growth as a designer, was the long, resonant essay with the learned title, « Consistent Correlation between Book Page and Type Area », included in the present volume. Tschichold was 60 when it was published, privately, in Basel in 1962. This crucial study has been reprinted in Germany many times, and there was an early English translation by Ruari McLean, published in 1963 as ‹ Non-arbitrary Proportions of Page and Type Area, › in the now-defunct trade journal *Print in Britain*. So far as I know, this is nevertheless the essay's first appearance in book form in English. (The only other among these essays which had previously appeared in English is ‹ Clay in a Potter's Hand, › translated in the *Penrose Annual*, London, 1949.)

Tschichold's writing, like his mind, covered considerable ground, yet it constantly returned to nagging details and root considerations of his chosen craft. His professional essays range from the broad principles of color and proportion in typography to the fine details of indenting paragraphs, spacing ellipses, and the forms of the ampersand (&) and eszett (ß). He translated not only T.J. Cobden-Sanderson but also Paul Valéry. He edited anthologies of calligraphic and typographic art, but also of German love poetry and of Persian verse in German translation. Besides his typographical books and essays, he wrote on Chinese woodblocks, Vietnamese folk art and the satirical novels of Laurence Sterne. The man expelled from his Munich teaching post by the Nazis because his gymnastic typographical designs ‹ threatened German morality and culture › was alert to the wisdom of Epiktetos, the freed Greek slave whom the Emperor Domitian had banished from Rome in A D 89 for teaching philosophy. Tschichold's favorite comic novelist quotes a statement by Epiktetos on the title page of volume one of *Tristram Shandy:* ‹Not things, but beliefs about things, plague humankind.›

Like his eminent contemporary Stanley Morison, Tschichold loved categorical statements and absolute rules, but he was vitally aware of their limitations. Time and again in these essays he delivers a rule with dictatorial pith and finality – and begins in the very next sentence to list the exceptions and contradictions. If, on occasion, he omits to list them, we owe him the courtesy of naming some ourselves. It was not his ambition to be God.

It was, however, his ambition to make visible the music of the spheres. *Harmonie* and *Takt* are words that appear repeatedly in some of these essays. The latter is often translated, correctly, as tact. But the German word has musical connotations which its English cognate lacks. *Takt* means measure, rhythm, time in the musical sense. A *Taktstock* is a conductor's baton. When Tschichold speaks of ‹harmonically perfect margins› or of ‹part-title pages in the same key as the text page›, and when he says that true book design ‹is a matter of *Takt* alone›, it is well to remember that the author of these phrases was born and raised in the shadow of Bach's Johanniskirche. Tschichold played no instrument himself except the typecase and the pencil, but these musical analogies are not sweet turns of phrase or platitudes; they reach deep into the craft.

Tschichold spent his working life not in devotion to the private press but in the world of perpetual compromise, otherwise known as trade publishing. His central task at Penguin Books and elsewhere, as he explained in another essay, was mass-producing the classics. He wanted, therefore, not only to design the perfect page but also to understand the inner grammar of his own design, in order to teach the basic principles to others. The reason was simple: he wanted not to take refuge in a better library but to live in a better world.

That desire underlies his insistence on reaching solutions by calculation instead of unquestioned rule or untracked instinct. The aim was not to disallow or discredit instinct, but to open instinct's eyes. Like any cook, Tschichold knew that components, conditions and occasions differ. Calculate the precise position, he says – and then make adjustments, if they are needed, using your educated eye. In the language of the kitchen: try the recipe or alter it as required to suit your ingredients and conditions, but in either case, taste the result and correct the seasoning while the chance is still at hand.

His first book, *Die Neue Typographie,* The New Typography (Berlin, 1928), preached the doctrine of economy, simplicity and functionalism, and attempted to find unifying principles linking every province of typographic design. A later book, *Typographische Gestaltung,* Typographic Configuration (Basel, 1935), which moderated and deepened these principles, nevertheless pursued the same agenda. Another of its themes was the relationship between modern typography and non-representational painting.

Typographische Gestaltung altered the practice of a whole new generation of designers when Ruari McLean's English translation was finally published in 1967, under the title *Asymmetric Typography.* The English-speaking world up to that point had been happy enough to flirt with European functionalist architecture and industrial design. Harvard, Yale, Aspen and Chicago had made a little room for Walter Gropius and other Bauhaus refugees. But North Americans were in no hurry to admit that books can be as important, or deserve as much respect, or be as demanding to design, as buildings. Our collective reluctance to think about typography may be measured in this case by two facts. First (though the Tschichold bibliographies* do not say so) the originating publisher of *Asymmetric Typography* was neither one of the large New York and London firms who eventually joined as copublishers; it was instead a small Canadian company of designers and typographers, Cooper & Beatty of Toronto. Second, when it was finally issued, that English translation had already existed in manuscript for more than twenty years.

In the meantime, Tschichold, like any self-respecting artist, had left his own manifesti and textbooks far behind. In fact, the asymmetrical, serifless radical began to do symmetrical, serifed design no later than 1935, the same year in which his brief on behalf of asymmetry was published in its original edition. Like Stravinsky, after making his reputation first as a rebel, he entered on a long and productive neoclassical phase.

That was the mode of design which he brought to Penguin Books, when he became Director of Typography there in 1947. During his two-year term, he educated the taste of a generation of readers both in Britain and overseas, and revolutionized the practice of a generation of otherwise happily inert British printers and typesetters as well. It was long after Tschichold's return to Switzerland in 1949 that Penguin Books underwent a partial conversion to the asymmetric, sanserif design he had been preaching in Munich and Basel decades before.

* Jan Tschichold: *Typograph and Schriftentwerfer. Zürich: Kunstgewerbemuseum, 1976, and* Leben und Werk des Typographen Jan Tschichold, *Dresden: Verlag der Kunst, 1977.*

The ornate yet corseted ugliness of European typography at the beginning of the twentieth century needed vigorous cleansing and exercise, and functionalist modernism appeared to be the goad and caustic required. This explains well enough the motivation behind the New Typography of the 1920s. But what were the motives of the neoclassicist modernism that followed? In 1946, in an essay entitled *Glaube und Wirklichkeit*, Faith and Fact,* Tschichold contemplated the meaning of his shifts in style:

Deriving typographical principles from what we used to call ‹abstract› or ‹nonobjective› painting ... gave us a suddenly strange and useful typography. Yet it seems to me no coincidence that this typography was almost wholly a German creation, little welcomed in other countries. Its impatient attitude stems from the German preference for the absolute.... I saw this only later, however, in democratic Switzerland. Since then I have ceased to promote the New Typography....

The Third Reich was second to none in pursuing technical ‹progress› through its preparations for war, which were hypocritically concealed behind the propaganda for medieval forms of society and expression. Deception lay at its root, and that is why it could not abide the honest modernists who were its political opponents. Yet they themselves, without knowing it, stood very close to the mania for ‹order› that ruled the Third Reich....

The New or Functional Typography is perfectly suited to advertising the products of industry (it has the same origin, after all), and it fulfills that function now as it did then. Its

* *A full English translation is published as Appendix 3 of Ruari McLean's useful book* Jan Tschichold: Typographer, *London: Lund Humphries, 1975.*

means of expression are nonetheless limited, because its only goal is zealous ‹clarity› or ‹purity› …. Bodoni was the ancestor of the New Typography insofar as he undertook to purge roman type of all traces of the underlying written forms and … to reconstruct it from simple geometrical shapes.

But many typographical problems cannot be solved along these regimented lines without doing violence to the text.…

The practical questions which flow from this realization are addressed by several essays in the present book: ‹Symmetrical or Asymmetrical Typography?›, ‹The Importance of Tradition in Typography›, and others, written in the 1950s and 1960s. The art historical questions – the questions of ethics and aesthetics and interpretation – which also flow from Tschichold's perceptive and courageous inquest into the meaning of typographic style, are questions every typographer, type designer and reader in the present day might wish to keep on asking, and trying to answer anew.

The designing of type, as distinct from designing *with* type, is a subject that doesn't arise in this book of essays, but type design was also an essential aspect of Tschichold's career. Unfortunately, his stature in this field is difficult to evaluate, because so much of the evidence has been destroyed. His early titling faces, designed for Lettergieterij Amsterdam and the Schelter & Giesecke foundry in Leipzig, are not of enduring interest. But the eight or ten serifed and unserifed text faces he designed for the Uhertype photosetting system in the 1930s were not put into production before the War, and all the artwork now appears to be lost. I have seen trial samples of the Uhertype sanserif roman that reveal it as a light and graceful font, possibly on a par with the best sanserifs of the day – Paul Renner's Futura and Eric Gill's

Gill Sans. If the other fonts were of equal merit, it would be well worth sifting the pieces and restoring these faces for use in the present day.

Tschichold's only surviving text family, Sabon, was drawn in the early 1960s. His commission in this case was to design a family of type for both hand and machine composition in metal. It was to echo the roman types of Claude Garamond, and its size and color were not to vary, regardless what method of composition was used. In other words, it had to meet the simultaneous technical constraints of Monotype and Linotype, and yet to look worthy of setting by hand. This placed complex limits on the character widths, the lengths of ascenders and descenders, the kerning possibilities, and other factors. But Tschichold thrived on such challenges. Sabon met the original demands and survived almost immediate translation to phototype. It remains an exemplary and useful face now, in the quaint new world of digital machines.

*

It was Vic Marks who originally insisted that an English edition of *The Form of the Book* ought to exist, and Hajo Hadeler who made the translation. My own contribution, which has been minimal, extends only to translating four lines of Heine, inserting a few dates, names and asterisks, and lobbying for the retention of Tschichold's duck feet to mark titles and quotations. The design of the book is based on Tschichold's own, though the scale is larger, and the texture of the page has changed. (The German original was set in Monotype Van Dijck.)

Tschichold planned to issue the first German edition of these essays in 1967, but publication was delayed until 1975, the year after his death. A second edition – our copy text for this translation – was published in 1987. Of the twenty-five essays in that volume, two seemed to me of little potential use or interest to the reader at the present day. One was devoted to spine lettering and the other to printers' signature marks. Both were short, and I have omitted them. In the essays that remain, I've also excised an occasional paragraph where the context seemed limited to the almost extinct phenomenon of commercial letterpress printing, or to specifically German and German-Swiss conditions. (Tschichold himself took the same approach when he was consulted about the English translation of *Typographische Gestaltung*.)

The text as it stands is still intimately involved with practical considerations. Letterpress and offset differ, as oil and watercolor do, and Tschichold was the kind of artist who works in close collaboration with his medium. His easy dismissal of marginal notes, and of hanging or outdented numbers, for example, can be traced in part to the economic constraints of commercial letterpress printing. In the world of digital page make-up, these particular constraints have disappeared, and others have replaced them. But the underlying logic, intelligence and spirit of Tschichold's approach to typography remains.

Because techniques and ideas change, I have tried to determine the date of first publication for each essay, and to record that date in the Table of Contents. So far as I can tell, the five essays dated 1975 remained unpublished until their posthumous inclusion in the first German edition of this book. I believe they were composed no later than 1967.

ROBERT BRINGHURST

THE FORM
OF THE BOOK

Clay in a Potter's Hand*

PERFECT typography is more a science than an art. Mastery of the trade is indispensable, but it isn't everything. Unerring taste, the hallmark of perfection, rests also upon a clear understanding of the laws of harmonious design. As a rule, impeccable taste springs partly from inborn sensitivity: from feeling. But feelings remain rather unproductive unless they can inspire a secure judgment. Feelings have to mature into knowledge about the consequences of formal decisions. For this reason, there are no born masters of typography, but self-education may lead in time to mastery.

It is wrong to say that there is no arguing about taste when it is good taste that is in question. We are not born with good taste, nor do we come into this world equipped with a real understanding of art. Merely to recognize who or what is represented in a picture has little to do with a real understanding of art. Neither has an uninformed opinion about the proportions of Roman letters. In any case, arguing is senseless. He who wants to convince has to do a better job than others.

Good taste and perfect typography are suprapersonal. Today, good taste is often erroneously rejected as old-fashioned because the ordinary man, seeking approval of his so-called personality, prefers to follow the dictates of his own

* *Written in England, late in 1948.* – J T

3

peculiar style rather than submit to any objective criterion of taste.

In a masterpiece of typography, the artist's signature has been eliminated. What some may praise as personal styles are in reality small and empty peculiarities, frequently damaging, that masquerade as innovations. Examples are the use of a single typeface – perhaps a sanserif font or a bizarre nineteenth-century script – a fondness for mixing unrelated fonts; or the application of seemingly courageous limitations, such as using a single size of type for an entire work, no matter how complex. Personal typography is defective typography. Only beginners and fools will insist on using it.

Perfect typography depends on perfect harmony between all of its elements. We must learn, and teach, what this means. Harmony is determined by relationships or proportions. Proportions are hidden everywhere: in the capaciousness of the margins, in the reciprocal relationships to each other of all four margins on the page of a book, in the relationship between leading of the type area and dimensions of the margins, in the placement of the page number relative to the type area, in the extent to which capital letters are spaced differently from the text, and not least, in the spacing of the words themselves. In short, affinities are hidden in any and all parts. Only through constant practice and strictest self-criticism may we develop a sense for a perfect piece of work. Unfortunately, most seem content with a middling performance. Careful spacing of words and the correct spacing of capital letters appear to be unknown or unimportant to some typesetters, yet for him who investigates, the correct rules are not difficult to discover.

Since typography appertains to each and all, it leaves no room for revolutionary changes. We cannot alter the essential shape of a single letter without at the same time destroying the familiar printed face of our language, and thereby rendering it useless.

Comfortable legibility is the absolute benchmark for all typography – yet only an accomplished reader can properly judge legibility. To be able to read a primer, or indeed a newspaper, does not make anyone a judge; as a rule, both are readable, though barely. They are *decipherable.* Decipherability and ideal legibility are opposites. Good legibility is a matter of combining a suitable script and an appropriate typesetting method. For perfect typography, an exhaustive knowledge of the historical development of the letters used in printing books is absolutely necessary. More valuable yet is a working knowledge of calligraphy.

The typography of most newspapers is decidedly backward. Lack of form destroys even the first signs of good taste and forestalls its development. Too lazy to think, many people read more newspapers than books. Small wonder, then, that typography as a whole is not evolving, and book typography is no exception. If a typesetter reads more newspapers than anything else, where would he acquire a knowledge of good taste in typography? Just as a person gets used to poor cuisine when nothing better is available and means of comparison are lacking, so many of today's readers have grown used to poor typography because they read more newspapers than books and thus *kill time,* as it is so succinctly termed. Since they aren't acquainted with better typography, they can't ask for it. And not knowing how to make things better, the rest lack voice.

Beginners and amateurs alike overestimate the importance of the so-called brain wave, the sudden brilliant idea. Perfect typography is largely a matter of choice among different and already existing possibilities: a choice based on vast experience. The correct choice is a question of tact. Good typography can never be humorous. It is precisely the opposite of an adventure. The brilliant idea counts for little or nothing at all. It counts the less, since it can only apply to a single job. It is a condition of good typographic work that each single part be formally dependent upon every other part. These relationships are developed slowly while the work is in progress. Today, the art of good typography is eminently logical. It differs from all other art forms in that a substantial portion of the inherent logic is accessible for verification by lay persons. Circumstances exist, however, where a perfectly logical but too complex graduation of type sizes may be sacrificed to achieve a simpler image.

The more significant the content of a book, the longer it has to be preserved, and the more balanced, indeed, the more perfect its typography has to be. Leading, letterspacing and word spacing must be faultless. The relationships of the margins to each other, the relationships of all type sizes used, the placement of running heads: everything must exhibit noble proportions and yield an unalterable effect.

The decisions made in *higher* typography – about the design of a book title, for example – are, like a highly refined taste, related to creative art. Here, forms and shapes may be invented which in their perfection are the equal of anything good sculpture and painting have to offer. The connoisseur is compelled to admire these creations all the more since the typographer is chained more than any other artist by the unalterable word, and only a master can awaken to their true life the rigid and formal letters used in the printing of books.

Immaculate typography is certainly the most brittle of all the arts. To create a whole from many petrified, disconnected and given parts, to make this whole appear alive and of a piece – only sculpture in stone approaches the unyielding stiffness of perfect typography. For most people, even impeccable typography does not hold any particular aesthetic appeal. In its inaccessibility, it resembles great music. Under the best of circumstances, it is gratefully accepted. To remain nameless and without specific appreciation, yet to have been of service to a valuable work and to the small number of visually sensitive readers – this, as a rule, is the only compensation for the long, and indeed never-ending, indenture of the typographer.

Graphic Arts and Book Design

THE WORK of a book designer differs essentially from that of a graphic artist. While the latter is constantly searching for new means of expression, driven at the very least by his desire for a ‹personal style›, a book designer has to be the loyal and tactful servant of the written word. It is his job to create a manner of presentation whose form neither overshadows nor patronizes the content. The work of the graphic artist must correspond to the needs of the day and, other than in collections, seldom lives on for any length of time – unlike a book, which is presumed to last. The aim of the graphic artist is self-expression, while the responsible book designer, conscious of his obligation, divests himself of this ambition. Book design is no field for those who desire to ‹mint the style of today› or to create something ‹new›. In the strict meaning of the word there cannot be anything ‹new› in the typography of books. Though largely forgotten today, methods and rules upon which it is impossible to improve have been developed over centuries. To produce perfect books, these rules have to be brought back to life and applied. The objective of all book design must be perfection: to find the perfect typographical representation for the content of the book at hand. To be ‹new› and surprising is the aim of advertising graphics.

The typography of books must not advertise. If it takes on elements of advertising graphics, it abuses the sanctity of the written word by coercing it to serve the vanity of a graphic artist incapable of discharging his duty as a mere lieutenant. This does not imply that the book designer's work must be colorless or empty of expression, nor that a book created anonymously in a print shop may not be beautiful. Thanks to the work of Stanley Morison, leading artist of the Monotype Corporation, London, England, the number of splendid publications has risen dramatically during the past twenty-five years.* Selecting a font absolutely in tune with the text; designing a consummate page with harmonically perfect margins, ideally legible, with immaculate word and letterspacing; choosing rhythmically correct type sizes for titles and headings; and composing genuinely beautiful and graceful part-title pages in the same key as the text page – by these means, a book designer can contribute much to the enjoyment of a valuable work of literature. If, instead, he chooses a currently trendy face, perhaps a sanserif or one of the not-always-ugly but for a book usually too obtrusive German ‹designer› foundry faces, then he turns the book into an article of fashion. This is proper only when the product at hand is short-lived. It is out of place when the book has any inherent importance. The more significant the book, the less room for the graphic artist to position himself and document through his ‹style› that he, and no one else, designed the book.

There is no doubt that works on new architecture or modern painting may derive their typographical style from current graphic art; yet these are the rarest of exceptions. Even for a book on Paul Klee, for instance, it does not seem right to use an ordinary industrial sanserif. Its poverty of expression will humiliate the subtlety of this painter. And to set

---

* *This statement was made in 1958. Morison, of course, was Monotype's typographical advisor and not himself an artist or designer. – R B*

9

a philosopher or a classical poet in this ostensibly modern font is out of the question. Book artists have to slough off their own personality completely. Above all they have to have a mature sense of literature and be able to estimate the importance of one piece of writing against another. Those who think in purely visual terms are useless as book designers. They routinely fail to see that their artful creations are signs of disrespect for the very literature they ought to serve.

True book design, therefore, is a matter of *tact* (tempo, rhythm, touch) alone. It flows from something rarely appreciated today: *good taste*. The book designer strives for perfection; yet every perfect thing lives somewhere in the neighborhood of dullness and is frequently mistaken for it by the insensitive. In a time that hungers for tangible novelties, dull perfection holds no advertising value at all. A really well-designed book is therefore recognizable as such only by a select few. The large majority of readers will have only a vague sense of its exceptional qualities. Even from the outside, a truly beautiful book cannot be a novelty. It must settle for mere perfection instead.

Only the book jacket offers the opportunity to let formal fantasy reign for a time. But it is no mistake to strive for an approximation between the typography of the jacket and that of the book. The jacket is first and foremost a small poster, an eye-catcher, where much is allowed that would be unseemly within the pages of the book itself. It is a pity that the cover, the true garb of a book, is so frequently neglected in favor of today's multicolored jacket. Perhaps for this reason many people have fallen into the bad habit of placing books on the shelf while still in their jackets. I could understand this if the cover were poorly designed or even repulsive. But as a rule, book jackets belong in the waste paper basket, like empty cigarette packages.

As for the book itself, it is the supreme duty of responsible designers to divest themselves of all ambition for self-expression. They are not the master of the written word but its humble servants.

On Typography

TYPOGRAPHY, even when poorly executed, can never be taken for granted; nor is it ever accidental. Indeed, beautifully typeset pages are always the result of long experience. Now and then they even attain the rank of great artistic achievement. But the art of typesetting stands apart from expressive artwork, because the appeal is not limited to a small circle. It is open to everyone's critical judgment, and nowhere does this judgment carry more weight. Typography that cannot be read by everybody is useless. Even for someone who constantly ponders matters of readability and legibility, it is difficult to determine whether something can be read with ease, but the average reader will rebel at once when the type is too small or otherwise irritates the eye; both are signs of a certain illegibility already.

All typography consists of letters. These appear either in the form of a smoothly running sentence or as an assembly of lines, which may even have contrasting shapes. Good typography begins, and this is no minor matter, with the typesetting of a single line of text in a book or a newspaper. Using exactly the same typeface, it is possible to create either a pleasant line, easily read, or an onerous one. Spacing, if it is too wide or too compressed, will spoil almost any typeface.

First and foremost, the form of the letters themselves contribute much to legibility or its opposite. Few people waste a thought on the form of a typeface. And for a lay person it is hardly possible to select, from the host of available typefaces, the one particular font suitable for the job at hand. Selection is not exclusively a question of taste.

The printed word addresses everybody, people of all ages, the educated and the less educated alike. He who can read enters into a contract that is more cohesive and more difficult to extinguish than any other. We cannot change the characteristics of a single letter without at the same time rendering the entire typeface alien and therefore useless. The more unusual the look of a word we have read – that is to say, recognized – a million times in familiar form, the more we will be disturbed if the form has been altered. Unconsciously, we demand the shape to which we have been accustomed. Anything else alienates us and makes reading difficult. We may conclude that a typeface is the more legible the less its basic form differs from what has been used for many generations. Small modifications are thinkable – form and lengths of the serifs, for instance, or an altered relationship between heavy and lighter parts of the letter. But these virtual variations find their limit in the contract established by the basic form of the letter.

Fifty years of experimentation with many novel, unusual scripts have yielded the insight that the best typefaces are either the classical fonts themselves (provided the punches or patterns have survived), or recuttings of these, or new typefaces not drastically different from the classical pattern. This is a late and expensive, yet still valuable, lesson. The noblest virtue of any script is not to be noticed as such. Really good typography should be legible after ten, fifty, even a hundred years and should never rebuff the reader. This cannot be said of all books printed in the past half-century. Many a variation can be understood only by those with knowledge of historical affinities. But in the endeavor to reform – and much was in need of reformation at the turn of the century – the mark has often been missed.

Looking back, it appears that above all people wanted things to be different. A new script was supposed to be noticeable as such, a personality craving respect. These conspicuous font personalities came in handy at a time when advertising was only primitively understood. Today the effect of most scripts that appeared before the First World War has worn off. Only a few can still be used.

The picture of typography around 1924 was that of a landscape carved up by the wish to create a new style, the *Stilwillen* of many and very dissimilar personalities. It suffered from a great number of disparate scripts. Typesetting machines – which today have a beneficial effect by helping to limit the number of fonts in use* – were few and far between. Almost everything was handset. Different fonts were available than in 1880, but they were not always better, and there were hardly any fewer. Thoughtless script mixtures sprouted like weeds. One of the pioneers of clean, strict typography at the time was Carl Ernst Poeschel, who, earlier than others, strove for typographical order. Though he used a number of fonts which today we would consider hideous, he still did excellent work. Then there was Jakob Hegner, who, thoughtfully using a selection of traditional typefaces, printed a large number of books that are still beautiful today.

The so-called New Typography appeared in 1925. It demanded radical simplicity and an abandonment of symmetrical composition. Thus it committed two errors in reasoning. First, it blamed the general confusion in the field solely on the

---

* *The date of this statement was 1952.* – R B

multitude of typefaces and claimed to have found the cure, the font for our time, in the sanserif. Second, it regarded the ‹center axis› (which had indeed led to some ridiculous creations) as a straitjacket and looked to asymmetry as a way out. Then as now, a strict reduction in the number of the roman and blackletter fonts used, retaining only the best of the available forms, and more exacting layout, would have sufficed to improve the image of typography considerably. The sanserif only seems to be the simpler script. It is a form that was violently reduced for little children. For adults it is more difficult to read than serifed roman type, whose serifs were never meant to be ornamental. Nor is asymmetry in any way better than symmetry; only different. Both arrangements can be good.

The New Typography left its mark in many new and not always better sanserif typefaces. Only much later did it arrive in England, Italy and the United States. In England it was rarely understood and hardly achieved any significance, even though run-of-the-mill English typography at that time was as much in need of cleaning up as the German had once been. In Italy and particularly in the United States, however, the New Typography found intelligent and imaginative disciples. In Germany, where it would soon have died a natural death anyway, the movement was strangled in 1933.

At the time, the foundries produced a great number of new unserifed fonts, and for a while no other typefaces were evident. Typographical experimentation continued, fruitful in part. One rarely achieves much with a single lucky stroke, though, and even a small improvement of typography from the ground up cannot be attained in a mere decade. A Chinese proverb says: *Steady labor produces a fine piece of work.*

Besides the many sanserifs, other scripts were produced

at the time which did not always follow the fads of fashion, and a few may survive for a while. Among the fonts for hand-setting, those developed by Emil Rudolf Weiss are likely the most valuable contribution to typography of the third decade of our century. Among the fonts developed for the various mechanical typesetting systems, those which have followed classical pattern will retain their merit: Walbaum roman, for example, and Walbaum Fraktur. There are several new cuts of old scripts, which were produced more or less faithfully from old printings. Today the insight prevails that the only really good scripts are those that have stayed close to the major incarnations of the classical patterns, just as they were handed down.

It is our task to select from these major representatives of classical script and their contemporary variations a reasonable, and preferably small, number. Many modern typefaces are nothing but disfigured deviations from old fonts. To distinguish between good shapes and defective ones, a superbly trained eye is required. Only the never-ending contemplation of the most excellent printed material of the past enables one to pass judgment.

A good example of print must be of noble design and be pleasing to the eye. Beyond that, it should not attract particular attention. Heavy and light elements must show measured proportions. Descenders should not be shortened, and the average distance between two letters must not be disproportionately compressed. Tight letterspacing has disfigured many modern scripts as well as a number of reproductions of older typefaces for which the original material is now lost.

Every type shop should have available at least one representative of old-style roman, complete with italics, in all sizes from 6-point upwards, including 9-point and 14-point, and up to 72-point. In addition, there should be a good Fraktur, also in all sizes, at the very least up to 36-point. It seems to me that a new-style roman (Bodoni for example) is a less urgent requirement than one of the styles developed during the transitional period (Baskerville for instance) – but there is no argument against Walbaum roman, which I consider superior to Bodoni, since more restrained. A good slab-serif, as well as a good sanserif, is probably necessary. Yet when a selection is made, one has to keep in mind the fonts already available in order to avoid inherently disharmonious mixtures.

A precondition for satisfactory finished work and for pleasant readability is the correct typesetting of each single line. Most typesetting in most countries is too loose. This defect is inherited from the nineteenth century, whose light, thin and pointed scripts almost demanded word spacing with en quads. Our own somewhat bolder scripts lose their line bond if this wide spacing is adopted. Three-to-em or even more compressed word spacing should be made the rule, unconditionally, and not in books alone. Unless the work consists of unusually long sentences, it is also unnecessary to increase the space after a period.

The beginnings of paragraphs must be indented. Paragraphs without indent (unfortunately the rule in Germany, and only there) are a bad habit and should be eliminated. The indention – usually one em – is the only sure way to indicate a paragraph. The eye, on reaching the end of a line, is too inert to recognize a tight exit – and in works without indents, even that frequently has to be produced as an afterthought from a flush ‹last› line. In order of importance, legibility and clarity have to come first; a smooth contour of the typeset page is of lesser importance. Therefore, typesetting without indentions is to be dismissed as an error.

In Fraktur, letterspacing is used to set words off from their neighbors. Formerly one used a different type as well, Schwabacher for example, or a larger size of Fraktur. Misled by Fraktur composition, some German typesetters use letterspacing for emphasis even in roman lowercase, rather than setting a word off with italics. To space out letters in roman lowercase is not correct. Emphasis in roman text has to be effected by using italic. Another way of distinguishing words is through use of small capitals, something Fraktur does not have. Small caps are superior to the semibold letters widely used in the German language area, where small caps are almost unknown. If they should be asked for, a deception is laboriously concocted by using a smaller size of capitals. It is very desirable, therefore, that the general use of small caps be encouraged. Moreover, the best machine fonts and the most important fonts for handsetting should be enriched with their own small caps.

It should be a rule that lowercase is never and under no circumstances to be letterspaced. The only exception is for emphasis in otherwise smooth Fraktur setting. All letterspacing despoils readability and the harmonious word image. The fact that letterspacing occurs so frequently in book titles, job printing and display types goes back to the time of the German classical authors, a period not exactly renowned for great typography. While spacing in Fraktur can be bearable if dictated by necessity, in roman and italic it turns into repulsive nonsense. Moreover, spaced typesetting is twice as expensive.

On the other hand, roman capital letters must always and under all circumstances be letterspaced, using a minimum of one-sixth their body size. This number, however, is no more than a general guide, since the spaces between capital letters have to be balanced against each other according to their optical values. It should be self-evident that spacing between words set entirely in uppercase must be wider than that between words set in lowercase. Frequently, however, one sees word spacing that is the same, *i.e.* too narrow, or much too wide. Letterspacing must be evident but it shouldn't be needlessly obtrusive.

That which we call typographic style is first and foremost determined by our way of life and our working conditions. For instance, we are no longer in a position to produce the rich and multicolored margins and backgrounds so common in the nineteenth century. They would be much too expensive. And chances are, there's no one left to set them. Further, our time is in short supply and we have to find an easier way. If it is too complicated, it cannot be modern.

Today more than ever before, simplicity is the mark of nobility in any piece of masterful work. If you have ever had a chance to observe a real master at work, you may have marvelled at how quick and easy everything looked. He seemed to ‹shake it out of his sleeve›. Laboriously trying first this, then that, is the way of a novice.

I have to say so much about the type typesetters use because without these types, and without knowing why and how they are used, no respectable piece of work can be produced. Hesitant fiddling with all manner of typefaces results in wasted time and expensive work. This concern is valid also when the design and execution of the work are done by different people. It is doubtful that a graphic artist who cannot also set type can come up with a good and useful typographic design. Planning and execution must go hand in hand.

If a type shop employs a designer, the artist must be completely conversant with the specific possibilities inherent in the available typefaces; and has to know what is simple to set, and what is difficult. And only if the designer's layout sketch is faultless will the typesetting be exactly what he had in mind. An ordinary draftsman who does not know intimately the uniquely pearling black-and-white of type and is unable to play perfectly on the instrument of typography will always end up surprised and disappointed. By the same token, even an average typesetter should be able to work effortlessly and fast from a good layout, which need not be perfectly clean nor intelligible to a lay person. It is likely that a master could compose even without a sketch if he had to, but as a rule he would do a sketch anyway, if only to avoid the resetting of even a single word. A master avoids any unnecessary motion.

There are works that demand more than the usual expenditure of time in design and/or execution. These will always be the exception. Perhaps an hour of design time is more expensive than an hour of typesetting, but even three meticulous sketches are still cheaper than three completed versions of typesetting.

Most of all, the design must flow from the spirit of typography instead of trying to emulate or surpass the effects of other graphic techniques, like lithography or drawing. Typography is an art in its own right and different from both. There are two famous specimens of type, both truly monuments of typographic art. The first is well and widely known, at least by name: the *Manuale tipografico* of Giambattista Bodoni (Parma, 1818). Only a few are familiar with the other one, even though technically and artistically it is far more astonishing. I mean the *Spécimen-Album* of Charles Derriey (Paris, 1862). It was set and printed in hundreds of brilliant colors, innumerable scripts and countless ornaments, tastefully done and executed with an unsurpassed exactitude in the registration of the many vivid shapes. A printer or designer might admire the work, yet real typography this is not. Rather, it is the deceptive imitation of lithographic effects using typography, a false victory of typography over lithography. The remnants of those erroneous efforts include the highly sensitive English script fonts that may still be found in our type drawers. They fake lithography and, for that reason, do not make good book fonts. Good book types are solid. Very fine hairlines and, what is worse, connected scripts, are not typographical.

Good typography has a simple structure. The centered line is a specific and indeed supremely important structural component in good typography. This pattern is as modern today as ever. A scribe, even when using a typewriter, does not like to center headlines, because it costs an effort to do it. Only in typography does this arrangement make sense. To center lines of different weight and type size one beneath the other is at the same time the simplest and the best typographical method, because the line spacing can be changed easily and quickly within the galley. Much of the art is hidden in the spacing of the lines. Lines placed vertically are not only difficult to read but also technically inferior because they are difficult to move inside the galley (not to mention oblique composition, which goes absolutely against the grain of good typesetting). Of course one can work with plaster of paris, but typography this is not.

Good typography is economical in both time and resources. Someone who can set a normal book, title pages excepted, using a single typeface including italics, knows his trade. Someone who sets up three galleys for a small print job or a simple title still has much to learn. However, someone who feels he may set a letterhead using only a single size of type should not think he has found the philosopher's stone. He confuses his own comfort with that of the reader and disregards the point that all copy includes elements of greater and lesser importance.

What we do, and how we do it, should always spring from obvious necessity. If we do not recognize or feel this necessity, something is wrong. Egg-dancing in the arena of good taste may look funny for a time, but the results will not last. A typesetter should be a master of the trade rather than a clown with a new prank for each new day.

The argument about symmetry and asymmetry is futile. They each have their own areas and special possibilities. One should not believe, however, that asymmetrical composition is unconditionally more modern or even absolutely better merely because it is younger. Even in the best of cases, asymmetry is in no way simpler or easier to set than symmetry, and to turn up one's nose at symmetrical typesetting because it seems antiquated is simply a sign of limited maturity. A catalog set asymmetrically may demonstrate military order. In a book set in this fashion, the flow of reading would be disrupted. Asymmetrical letterheads may be better than symmetrical ones, but asymmetrical small advertisements look terrible when they are combined on a page. In typography neither the old style nor a new style matters; quality does.

The Importance of Tradition
in Typography*

M A N Y buildings and everyday objects are unmistakable doc-
uments of the present. As building methods changed, so did
architecture. As material and production methods changed,
so did the shape of most tools and utensils. In these areas tradition has become meaningless; today's buildings and many
of the things we use every day have no tradition apart from
the short span of a few decades.

The elements and form of a book and of much other
printed matter, however, are clearly derived from the past,
even when mass production causes millions of copies to be
printed. The *Roman* gestalt of the written word irrevocably
ties the education and culture of every single human being to
the past, whether he is conscious of it or not. That we have to
thank the Renaissance for today's printing type – indeed,
that the very typefaces used today are often Renaissance faces
– is either unknown or of no consequence to most people.
The average man accepts letters as common and given sym-
bols of communication.

All typography implies tradition and conventions. *Tradi-
tio* derives from Latin *trado,* I hand over. Tradition means
handing over, delivering up, legacy, education, guidance.

* This essay was presented as a lecture by the author at the 200th anniver-
sary of the Hochschule für Graphik und Buchkunst, *Leipzig, October 9,*
1964. – J T

Convention derives from *convenio,* to come together, and means agreement. I use the word *convention* and its derivative, *conventional,* only in its original and never in any derogatory sense.

The form of our letters, the older handwriting and inscriptions as much as the cuttings in use today, reflects a convention that has slowly solidified, an agreement hardened in many battles. Even after the Renaissance several European countries retained broken, blackletter national scripts in opposition to roman, the obligatory type for all Latin material; yet even today, I hope, the last word about Fraktur has not been spoken. Apart from that, the roman minuscule has been our way of writing for hundreds of years. What followed were merely fashionable variations, here and there even deformations, of the noble basic form, but no improvement whatever. The punches of Claude Garamond, cut around 1530 in Paris, are simply unsurpassed in their clarity, readability and beauty. Garamond appeared on the scene at a time when the occidental book, as an object, cast off its medieval ponderousness and took up the form which today is still the best: the slender and upright rectangular body, comprising folded sheets stitched or sewn at the back, in a cover whose protruding edges protect the trimmed pages.

For about one hundred and fifty years the shape of the book has been manipulated in multifarious ways. First, the typefaces used became pointed and thin; next came a deliberate broadening of the body, reducing its compactness. Later the paper was smoothed to such a degree that the fibres and thus the durability of the book began to suffer. Then came the attempts at reform by William Morris and his imitators in England, and finally there appeared the German script artists of the first three decades of our century, whose new typefaces are now largely forgotten.

Interesting as they may be for the historian and collector, and notwithstanding the fact that at the time here and there something valid, even something noteworthy, was created, all these experiments have only one reason: discontent with what existed. Even the attempt to deliberately create something new or at least something different is legitimized first and foremost by this dissatisfaction. Lack of pleasure in the usual, the commonplace, deludes one into the dark notion that different could be better. One finds something bad, is unable to pin down why it is so, and simply wants to do something different. Trendy ideas about shape and form, inferiority complexes and new technical possibilities all play a role, but they are weaker forces than the protest of the young against the ways of the older generation. Granted, such protest against established shape and form almost always has a good reason behind it, and the truly perfect is rare indeed! But any protest must remain infertile, and achievements based on protest must remain open to question, as long as the apprenticeship is incomplete and the typographical grammar has not been studied thoroughly. This schooling alone gives us the tools for constructive criticism, for understanding.

What really counts in the typesetter's art is what everybody looks at every day: first, picturebook and primer; next, the reader, the textbook, the novel, the newspaper, the printed material of every day. And there is very little among it whose shape and form brings us even so much as a little joy. And yet, it is no more costly to produce a good children's book or to typeset a novel really well than to do the commonplace, the usual. It is indeed true that something is wrong with so many printed works. But, without researching methodically the causes of the wrongness, without being properly equipped for such an analysis, the naïve person believes that making it different is making it better. What is more, there are always people around offering ever-simpler recipes as the last word in wisdom. At the present it is the ragged-right line, in an unserifed face, and preferably in one size only.

The real reason for the number of deficiencies in books and other printed matter is the lack of – or the deliberate dispensation with – tradition, and the arrogant disdain for all convention. If we can comfortably read anything at all, it is exactly because we respect the usual, the commonplace. To be able to read implies conventions, knowledge of them, and regard for them. If conventions are thrown overboard, the danger arises that the text will become unreadable. Case in point: the incomparably beautiful manuscripts of the Middle Ages are more difficult to read than our own books, even with a good knowledge of Latin, because their text format does not correspond with our habits; and a book written in Gabelsberger Stenography* is totally useless today because we can no longer read a single word of it. The use of conventional letters and of conventional spelling and style are unconditional prerequisites of generally comprehensible, *i.e.* useful, typography. One who pays no heed to this rule commits an offence against the reader.

This truth compels us first to look at the form of individual letters. The history of type design embraces thousands of different alphabets of very differing qualities which all derive from humanist roman, the Renaissance minuscule, the crys-

---

* *The shorthand system of Franz Xavier Gabelsberger, published in Germany in 1841.* – R B

tallized, final form of our script. Formal beauty is only one criterion, and hardly the most important one. Besides an indispensable rhythm, the most important thing is distinct, clear and unmistakable form: the highly sensitive, correct relationship of assimilation and distinction in each individual letter. It is the similarity of all letters, yet at the same time the distinctiveness of each individual symbol, that yields perfect readability. The faultless form of our letters is, as already mentioned, the work of the great typecutter Garamond. For a quarter of a millennium his was the only roman in Europe, if we disregard the countless imitations. We can read old books of the period as comfortably as our ancestors did, and easier than much of what we come across today. This is so, despite the fact that not all of the old books were set with the exquisite care demanded by today's expert. Rough paper and a not-always-flawless printing technique hide the imperfections. Good typesetting is tight. Generous letterspacing is difficult to read because the holes disturb the internal linking of the line and thus endanger comprehension of the thought. Consistent line spacing is easy to achieve with today's typesetting machines. Every single book printed before 1770 shows how correctly a compositor could work with type and line spacing. The idea of a ‹limited edition›, a connoisseur's book, was practically unknown. By and large the quality is uniform and high. It is as easy today to find an ugly book (take the first one that is handy) as it is difficult to discover a truly ugly old book from before 1770.

   In a pathological pursuit of things different, the reasonable proportions of paper size, like so many other qualities, have been banished by some to the disadvantage of the solitary and defenseless reader. There was a time when deviations from the truly beautiful page proportions 2:3, 1: $\sqrt{3}$, and the

Golden Section were rare. Many books produced between 1550 and 1770 show these proportions exactly, to within half a millimetre.

To learn this, one has to examine old books thoroughly. Alas, almost no one does this any more, yet the benefits of such study are immeasurable. Schools of typography, in cooperation with libraries of old books, need to undertake two things: first, a detailed inspection of old books, and second, in support of this, permanent as well as changing exhibitions of these old treasures. An admiringly superficial look at a particularly beautiful set of pages or title pages only is not sufficient. One has to be able to touch these books and carefully study their typographical structure page by page. Even old books whose content is no longer relevant can serve this purpose. It is true, we are born with our eyes, but they will only open slowly to beauty, much more slowly than one thinks. Nor is it simple to find a knowledgeable person one could ask for guidance. Frequently, a general educational background is lacking, even in the teacher.

Around 1930 a teacher of fine arts was outraged by the fact that a typographer was expected to know his way around in the history of script of the past two thousand years. By the way, demands in those days were more moderate than they are today. If we were to disregard such standards altogether, however, we would return to barbarism. He who no longer understands what he is doing is become as sounding brass or a tinkling cymbal.

Among old books one also does not find the unreasonable formats which are often presented to us today as works of the book maker's art. Large formats do indeed exist, but always for good reason – never born out of vanity or greed but always from plausible necessity. Enormous table-top tomes, similar to the pompous horrors of today and unsuited for reading, were occasionally produced for kings, but they are the rarest of exceptions. The reasonable format of the old books is exemplary.

A penetrating look at the books of the Renaissance, the golden age of book printing, and of the Baroque, will teach us best about the reasonable organization of a book. Frequently such a book is easier to read than many a work of the present. We look at wonderfully smooth typesetting, clearly structured into paragraphs (longer at that time), which always begin with an em-quad indent. To mark *Roman* caesuras, breaks or paragraphs in this manner was originally an accidental discovery, but it is the only good method. It has been used for hundreds of years until this very day. Now some people believe that the method is no longer modern and begin their paragraphs bluntly, flush left. This is simply wrong, because it obliterates the quintessential structure, which should be recognizable at the left-hand side of the type area. The quad indent is one of the most precious legacies of typographical - history.

Further, we see the beginnings of chapters emphasized by large capital letters, by initials. While these are also ornaments, first and foremost they serve to distinguish important starting points. Today they have almost fallen into disrepute, but they should be used again, at least in the form of large letters without decoration. Abandoning the use of these initial letters does not exempt us from the necessity to mark the opening of a new chapter effectively, perhaps by setting the first word with a capital and small caps, preferably without indention. An indent is senseless anyway when the heading is centered. It is not sufficient to emphasize major divisions within a chapter simply by inserting a blank line. How often does it happen that the last line of a major division is also the last line on a page! Therefore, at a minimum the first line of the new division should begin flush left and the first word be set with capital and small caps. Better still to insert a centered asterisk.

The Renaissance did not know our fear of oversize headings, which is so common today. Frequently, these large headings are set not in uppercase but in lowercase letters: a custom worth emulating. For fear of doing something wrong, one is too timid today in the selection of body sizes for the major lines of a title. On the other hand, the publishers' emblems or logos today are mostly small and do not permit a proper balance if the upper lines want to be really big.

In particular, a Renaissance book can teach us about the reasonable use of italic, either for distinguishing a passage of text or as the type for the foreword. It can teach us further about the proper use and setting of small caps, the sensible indention of continuing lines in the table of contents, and infinitely more.

Then there is the matter of positioning the type area convincingly on the page. Renaissance practice is not at all antiquated and, moreover, cannot be improved upon. The well-thought-out compactness of the finished book, the harmonious blend of printer's ink with the natural paper (which is not blinding white) should also be applauded.

While the old system of centered typesetting relates to the sense of order that prevailed during the Renaissance, it is nonetheless timeless. After centered primary and secondary headings, we can move headings of the last order over to the left. Clearly, this method is richer and more useful than a system that abandons all centering and tries to emphasize headings with semibold letters.

The typography of old books is a precious legacy, well worthy of continuation. It would be both impertinent and senseless to alter drastically the form of the European book. What has proved practical and correct over centuries, like the quad indent – should this be displaced by a so-called ‹experimental typography›? Only indisputable improvements would make sense. Real and true experiments have a purpose: they serve research, they are the means to find the truth and lead to evidence and proof. In themselves, experiments are not art. Infinite amounts of energy are wasted because everybody feels he has to make his own start, his own beginning, instead of getting to know what has already been done. It is doubtful that anyone who doesn't want to be an apprentice will ever become a master. To respect tradition is not at all historicism. All historicism is dead. But the best lettercutting of the past lives on. Two or three old designs are only waiting to be resurrected.

Typography is both art and science. Apparent knowledge, based on what has been handed down from one student to the next, like copies of copies of flawed later editions (rather than the immediate study of the originals), does not bring forth anything worthwhile. While typography is closely connected with technical machinery, technique alone does not originate art.

The tradition I am talking about here does not stand on the work of the immediately preceding generation, even though they are frequently congruent. We have to return to the great traditions of the Renaissance and the Baroque book, study the originals and fill them with new life. Here alone is the measuring stick by which we should methodically judge faulty books. Experiments aimed at creating something ‹different› may be fascinating and entertaining, at least for the experimenter. But a lasting tradition will not spring from experiments. Only the legacy of true mastery can provide this.

Ars typographica Lipsiensis vivat et floreat!

Symmetrical or
Asymmetrical Typography?

THE QUESTION, asked in this form, demands an explanation first. The word symmetrical may not be used when we
talk about a typographical arrangement, because something
is symmetrical only if one half is the mirror image of the other
half. Originally, the word meant balance in general. Over
time the meaning has narrowed down to that mentioned above.
Strictly symmetrical things do not necessarily have to be ugly,
but they are rarely beautiful. If we remember an old clothes
chest with a real keyhole on the right and a false one on the
left side: there was a time when the false keyhole would have
been missed.

Because the left half of a centered title or even of a single
line is not the mirror image of the right half, in the strictest
sense the entire composition is not symmetrical. There is no
such thing as symmetrical typography. When the lines are
justified towards the middle, we should call it centered typography. Not to mention that there is no such thing as a center axis, and therefore no *center axis typography* either. The
phrase *center axis* is a tautology. An axis is always the pivot of
that which turns around it, even if the structure itself is not
symmetrical.

A frame around typeset matter is symmetrical as a rule,
but it is an addition that need not be discussed here.

Countless natural forms appear symmetrical: the human
shape, the animal, a plant seed and an egg. Others develop towards general symmetry: a free-standing tree for instance.

The symmetrical appearance of a human being is reflected in the symmetrical shape of a book and even in a book title, where the lines have been centered. Similarly, the symmetrical architecture of the Renaissance is a response to the symmetrical appearance of man. In itself, a symmetrical arrangement is neither the mark of a particular style nor the expression of society, but rather a shape that grew almost naturally, a form that has been around at all times and in the most diverse societies. It is a visible effort toward order, toward a center; that is all it attests to.

What is it that causes so many symmetrical and quasi-symmetrical shapes to appear beautiful to our eyes?

Empty, a Rococo park, with its strict regularity, is unbearably stilted and dreary. Let a human being or a couple stroll around in it and the contrast between geometrical strictness and living movement brings it to life and renders the whole very pleasant.

A human being looks symmetrical from the outside, but the two halves of his face are never really symmetrical; more often than not, they are quite different. This difference is, at minimum, expressive and at times the real cause of beauty. A pebble gives us pleasure when it rolls like a ball. Expression and life mean motion. Immobile symmetry holds no tension and leaves us cold.

A richly decorated Baroque picture frame, or any other symmetrically structured ornamental border that appears beautiful to our eyes, may achieve this effect only because the motion inherent in the ornamentation disturbs the otherwise static picture.

Indeed, disturbance of perfect symmetry is one of the prerequisites for beauty. Anything not quite symmetrical is considerably more beautiful than faultless symmetry. In art, a nude is never portrayed standing at attention, but rather in a non-symmetrical position; this disarrangement of symmetry is indispensable.

In the same way, a quasi-symmetrical book title is beautiful and full of expression thanks to the subconsciously perceived tension between the asymmetrical word images and lines and the desire to enfold these elements and bind them to a symmetrical order. On the other hand, the appearance of perfectly symmetrical and static letters like A H M T V within the otherwise dynamically ordered typography on a page provides a pleasant retarding force.

Even a fluctuation between apparent symmetry and dynamic order can at times be gratifying, in a magazine, for instance; but to achieve this, a large measure of masterful certainty is required. There is no prescription that automatically produces art. Recent examples from the job-printing market demonstrate that a naturally centered typography may be abused and forced to assume attitudes of vanity, which are alien to printing. The result is no more than a fashionable craze.

Typography is a servant, not a master; the right gesture is invariably defined by expediency. It is therefore not inconsistent, and frequently advisable, to begin a book with a centered title and to place the chapter headings also in the middle. Subheadings, then, may be moved to the left.

As we can see, there is no real disparity between apparently symmetrical typography and the uncentered kind. What we have instead is a wide range of efforts that result in typography where either a centered composition or a dynamic one dominates. These arrangements and all their varieties may be suitable for the job at hand, or they may not. We can only hope that the results in each case are beautiful.

Consistent Correlation Between
Book Page and Type Area

TWO CONSTANTS reign over the proportions of a well-made book: the hand and the eye. A healthy eye is always about two spans away from the book page, and all people hold a book in the same manner.

The format of a book is determined by its purpose. It relates to the average size and the hands of an adult. Children's books should not be produced in folio size because for a child this format is not handy. A high degree or at least a sufficient degree of handiness has to be expected: a book the size of a table is an absurdity, books the size of postage stamps are trivialities. Likewise, books that are very heavy are not welcome; older people may not be able to move them around without help. Giants should have books and newspapers that are larger; many of our books would be too large for dwarfs.

There are two major categories of books: those we place on a table for serious study, and those we read while leaning back in a chair, in an easy chair, or while travelling by train. The books we study should rest at a slant in front of us. Few, however, will go to such length. To bend over a book is just as unhealthy as the usual writing position enforced by a flat table. The scribe of the middle ages used a desk; we hardly dare call it that any more because the slope was so steep (up to 65°). The parchment was held in place by a string across it and could be pushed upward little by little. The active line, always horizontal, was at height-of-eye, and the scribe sat perfectly upright. Even at the turn of the century, clergymen and government officials used to do their writing standing up behind a small desk: a healthy and reasonable position for writing and reading that has, alas, become rare.

The reading position has nothing to do with the size and dimension of textbooks. Their formats range from large octavo to large quarto. Still larger formats are the exception. Textbooks and coffee-table books rest on a desk. They cannot be read freehand.

Those books we like to hold in our hands while reading come in a variety of formats, all based on octavo. Even smaller books can be perfect provided they are slim; without effort they can be held for hours in one hand.

Only during church service do we see someone read from a book that has been set up: the reader's eyes may be at arm's length from the letters of the text. An ordinary book page is only a forearm's length from the eye of the reader. We are talking here about profane books only; not all of the following considerations and rules apply to sacred books as well.

Book pages come in many proportions, *i.e.* relationships between width and height. Everybody knows, at least from hearsay, the proportion of the Golden Section, exactly 1:1.618. A ratio of 5:8 is no more than an approximation of the Golden Section. It would be difficult to maintain the same opinion about a ratio of 2:3. In addition to the ratios of 1:1.618, 5:8 and 2:3, for books the ratios of 1:1.732 (1: $\sqrt{3}$) and 1:1.414 (1: $\sqrt{2}$) are used (see figure 18).

Figure 1 shows a little-known, very beautiful rectangle, derived from the pentagon (proportion 1:1.538).

The geometrically definable irrational page proportions like 1:1.618 (Golden Section), 1: $\sqrt{2}$, 1: $\sqrt{3}$, 1: $\sqrt{5}$, 1:1.538 (figure 1), and the simple rational proportions of 1:2, 2:3,

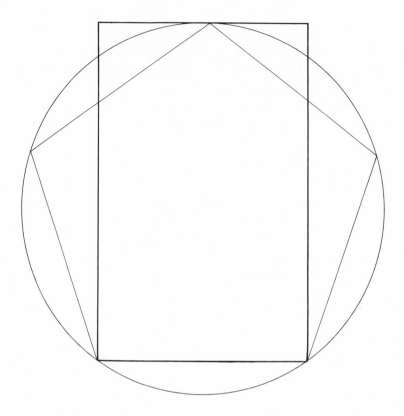

Figure 1. Rectangle, derived from a pentagon.
Proportion 1:1.538 (irrational).

5:8 and 5:9 I call clear, intentional and definite. All others are unclear and accidental ratios. The difference between a clear and an unclear ratio, though frequently slight, is noticeable.

Many books show none of the clear proportions, but accidental ones. We do not know why, but we can demonstrate that a human being finds planes of definite and intentional proportions more pleasant or more beautiful than those of accidental proportions. An ugly format causes an ugly book.

Since utility and beauty of all printed matter, whether book or flyer, ultimately depends on the page ratio of the paper size used, someone wanting to make a beautiful and pleasant book first has to determine a format of definite proportions.

However, a single definite ratio like 2:3, 1:1.414 or 3:4 is not adequate for all kinds of books. Once again it is the purpose which determines not only the size of the book but also the page proportions. The wide ratio of 3:4 is very well suited to books in quarto format because they rest on a table. The same proportion of 3:4 would make a small pocket book both unhandy and unseemly; even if it were not particularly heavy, we could hold it with one hand for only a short time, and in any case, the two halves of the book would always fall backward: such a book is much too wide. The same applies to books in A5 format (14.8 × 21 cm; 5⅞ × 8¼ in, 1: $\sqrt{2}$), unfortunately not so rare. A small or free-hand book has to be slim if we want to handle it easily. A ratio of 3:4 would not be suitable; one of the following proportions is better: 1:1.732 (very slim), 3:5, 1:1.618, or 2:3.

Small books have to be slim; large books may be wide. The small ones we hold in one hand; the large books rest on the table. The old sheet formats, all about 3:4 in proportion, when folded yield ratios of 2:4 and 3:4 in succession; the quarter-sheet is quarto or 3:4, the eighth is octavo or 2:3. The two major proportions of 2:3 (octavo) and 3:4 (quarto) form a sensible couple, like man and wife. The attempt to push them aside with the help of so-called normal formats, which use the hybrid ratio of 1: $\sqrt{2}$, goes against nature, like the wish to cancel the polarity of the sexes.

The new DIN raw sheet formats avoid the alternation of ratios 3:4 / 2:3 / 3:4 / 2:3 and retain their original proportion when halved. This ratio is 1:1.414. Sheets which, because of

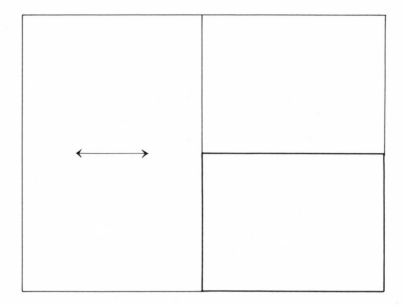

Figure 2. Quarto format, direction of grain shown.

their grain, are suitable for quarto, I cannot use for octavo books, because the grain would run the wrong way. Nor can I use them for *sextodecimo* books (1 sheet = 16 leaves or 32 pages) because the signature would be too thick. It follows that we would do just fine without the sheet proportion of 1:1.414 (see also figures 2 and 3).

The A4 format (21 × 29.7 cm; 8¼ × 11¾ in.) is well suited for two-column typesetting of magazines, for which even A5 (14.8 × 21 cm; 5⅞ × 8¼ in.) may be adequate; single-column typesetting on the other hand is seldom satisfactory in either format. Moreover, A5 is unpleasant when hand held, because it is too wide, too unwieldy and inelegant. The book proportion of 1:1.414 has existed once before, during the High Middle Ages, when many books were writ-

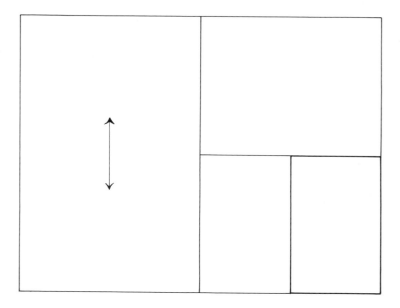

Figure 3. Octavo format requires the other grain direction.

ten with two columns. Gutenberg, however, preferred the page proportion of 2:3. During the Renaissance we seldom discover the ratio of 1:1.414. On the other hand, we spot numerous definitely slim volumes of great elegance, which should be our exemplars.

Except for the four-column *Codex Sinaiticus* in the British Museum, one of the oldest books in the world, there have been few square books. There is no need for them. As textbooks they are needlessly low and of irksome width; as handheld books they are unwieldy and more clumsy than any other format. During the Biedermeier era, a sedate and comfort-loving period, when typography and the art of making books began to fall apart, nearly square quarto and very wide octavo formats were not uncommon.

Around the turn of the century it became apparent how hideous books had become during the Biedermeier period. The type area was centered in the middle of the page, and the four margins were of equal width. All connection was lost between the pairs of pages, and they fell apart. The problem of a relationship between the four margins finally had become obvious, and rightly so. A solution was sought through use of numerical values.

However, these efforts took the wrong direction. Only under certain circumstances may the margins form a rational sequence (one expressible in simple numbers) such as 2:3:4:6 (inner margin to upper to fore-edge to foot). A margin progression of 2:3:4:6 is only possible with a sheet proportion of 2:3, and the typesetting format has to follow suit. If another sheet format proportion is being used, say $1: \sqrt{2}$, then a margin progression of 2:3:4:6 leads to a type area proportion different from that of the page proportion and therefore disharmonious. The secret of a harmonious book page is not necessarily hidden in a relationship between the four margins expressible in simple numbers.

Harmony between page size and type area is achieved when both have the same proportions. If efforts are successful to combine page format and type area into an indissoluble unit, then the margin proportions become functions of page format and overall construction and thus are inseparable from either. Margin proportions do not dominate the page of a book. Rather, they arise from the page format and the law of form, the canon. And what does this canon look like?

Before the printing process was invented, books were written by hand. Gutenberg and other early printers perused the written book as an example. Printers took over the laws of book form which the scribes had been following. It is cer-

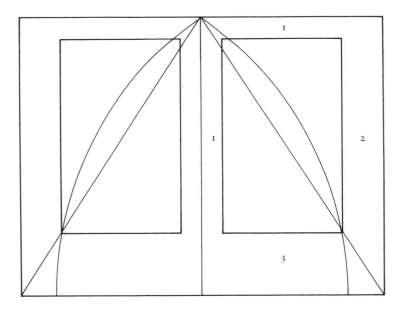

Figure 4. Framework of ideal proportions in a medieval manuscript without multiple columns. Determined by Jan Tschichold, 1953. Page proportion 2:3. Margin proportions 1:1:2:3. Text area proportioned in the Golden Section! The lower outer corner of the text area is fixed by a diagonal as well.

tain that there existed fundamental codes. Numerous medieval books show a surprising conformity in proportions of format and position of type area. Unfortunately, such codes have not come down to us. They were workshop secrets. Only by carefully measuring medieval manuscripts can we attempt to track them down.

Nor did Gutenberg himself invent a new law of form. He used the shop secrets of the initiated and followed in their footsteps. Presumably, Peter Schöffer had his hand in it as well. Superb calligrapher that he was, it may be presumed

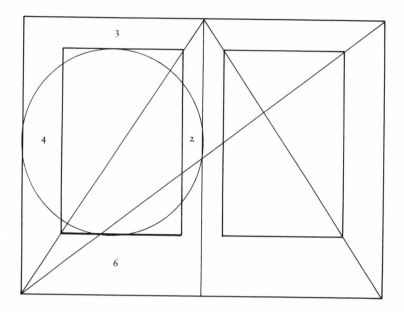

Figure 5. The secret canon, upon which many late medieval manu-
scripts and incunabula are based. Determined by Jan Tschichold,
1953. Page proportion 2:3. Text area and page show the same
proportions. Height of text area equals page width.
Margin proportions 2:3:4:6.

that he was conversant with these Gothic workshop secrets.

I have measured a great number of medieval manuscripts. Not every single one follows a code exactly; artlessly made books are no prerogative of our time. Discarding those, we only count manuscripts that were obviously produced thoughtfully and artfully.

After much toilsome work I finally succeeded, in 1953, in reconstructing the Golden Canon of book page construction as it was used during late Gothic times by the finest of scribes. It may be seen in figure 5. The canon in figure 4 I abstracted from manuscripts that are older yet. While beautiful, it would hardly be useful today. In figure 5 the height of the type area equals the width of the page: using a page proportion of 2:3, a condition for this canon, we get one-ninth of the paper width for the inner margin, two-ninths for the outer or fore-edge margin, one-ninth of the paper height for the top, and two-ninths for the bottom margin. Type area and paper size are of equal proportions. There have been other schemes, empirically developed, where equal proportions of type area and page format have been postulated. What had been missing, however, was the *use of the diagonal of the double page spread,* which here for the first time becomes an integral part of the construction.

What I uncovered as the canon of the manuscript writers, Raúl Rosarivo proved to have been Gutenberg's canon as well. He finds the size and position of the type area by dividing the page diagonal into ninths (figure 6).

The key to this positioning of the type area is the division into nine parts of both the width and the height of the page. The simplest way to do this was found by J. A. van de Graaf and is shown in figure 7. His method results in my own figure 5, and figure 6 of Rosarivo. For purposes of better comparison I have based his figure on a page proportion of 2:3, which van de Graaf does not use.

The final and most rewarding confirmation of my results as shown in figure 5 came from Villard's Diagram, inscribed in figure 8. This so far little known and truly exciting Gothic canon results in harmonious divisions and may be drawn into any rectangle whatever. Without use of a scale, a line may be divided into any number of equal parts. Figure 9 shows Villard's Diagram once again.

Raúl Rosarivo's investigations have proved the validity

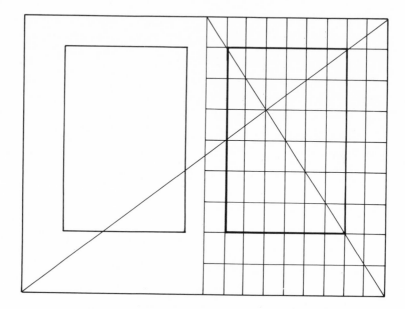

Figure 6. Division of height and width of a page into nine parts, following Rosarivo's construction. Like figure 5, this involves a 2:3 page proportion. The end result is congruent with figure 5; only the methods differ. This proved to be the canon used by Gutenberg and Peter Schöffer.

of the late-medieval scribe's canon as determined by myself for the first printers and thus corroborated its accuracy and its importance. However, we must not believe that the format ratio of 2:3, which belongs to this canon, was sufficient to meet all requirements. The late medieval period demanded neither particular convenience nor elegance from a book. Only much later, during the Renaissance, books were produced that were delicate as well as lightweight and handy. Little by little books appeared in smaller formats and in pro-

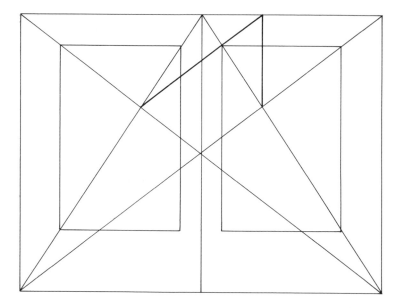

Figure 7. Division into nine parts, after van de Graaf, using a page proportion of 2:3. The simplest way to achieve the canon in figure 5. Compass and ruler instead of computations.

portions which are still conventional today: 5:8, 21:34, 1:$\sqrt{3}$, and the quarto format, 3:4. As beautiful as the ratio of 2:3 may be, it cannot serve for any and all books. Purpose and character of the work frequently demand another good proportion.

But the canon in figure 5 works for other format proportions as well. Used for any book format, it will invariably result in a non-random and harmonious position of the type area. Even the relative size of the type area may be altered without destroying the harmony of the book page.

Let us have a look first at the book formats of the Golden

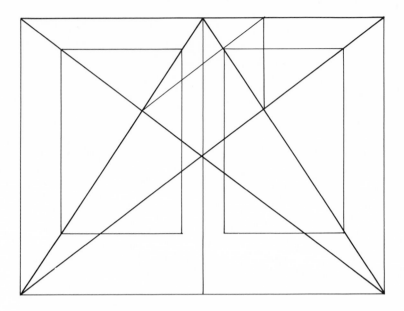

Figure 8. Villard's Diagram. Included in our page construction plan there is also a variation on Villard's Diagram. This is a canon of harmonious division named after its inventor, Villard de Honnecourt, an architect who lived and worked during the first half of the thirteenth century in the Picardy region of Northern France. His manuscript Bauhüttenbuch (*workshop record book*) *is held at the National Library in Paris. Using Villard's canon, shown in bold, it is possible to divide a straight line into any number of equal parts without need of a measuring stick.*

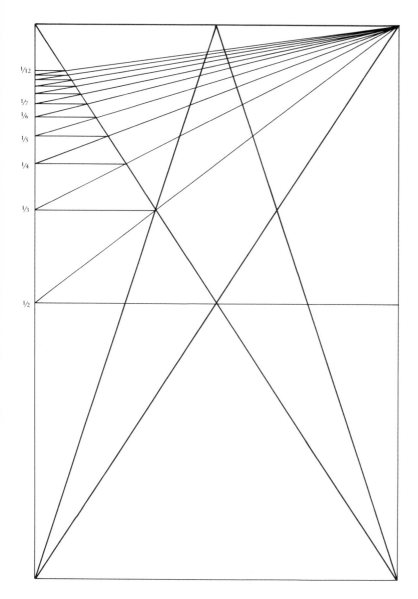

Figure 9. Villard's Figure, inscribed in a rectangle of 2:3 proportion.
The longer side divided down to a twelfth part.

49

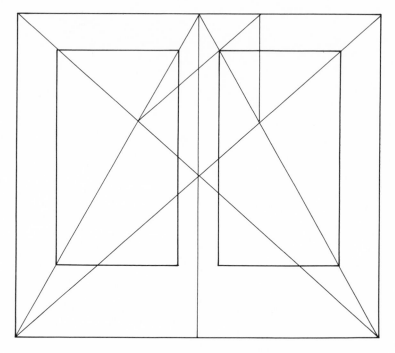

Figure 10. Page proportion 1: √3 (1:1.732). Division into ninths of both height and width of the paper.

Section and the proportions 1: √3, 1: √2, and quarto (3:4). We shall use the division into ninths, as developed in figure 5. Figures 10–13 show the application of Villard's Diagram as well, which may be drawn into any rectangle. Figures 14 and 15, square format and landscape, demonstrate how we arrive at harmonious and nonarbitrary type areas even when using unusual formats. A landscape arrangement is suitable for music books, for example, and for books containing pictures in oblong horizontal format. In most cases a page proportion of 4:3 works better than 3:2, which is too low.

Even the division into ninths, while no doubt the most

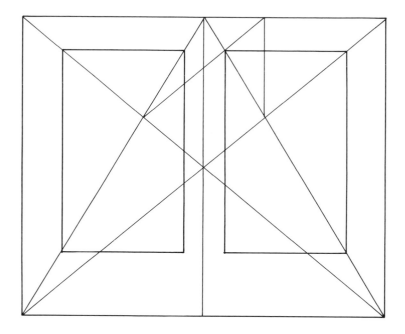

Figure 11. The page proportion of the Golden Section (21:34).
Paper height and width are divided into ninths. (For page
proportion of 2:3, see figures 5 through 7.)

beautiful, is not the only correct one. Dividing into twelfths
we get, as shown in figure 16, a larger type area when compared with figure 5. Figure 17 shows a sample of division into
sixths based on a page proportion of 2:3, after a small Italian
prayer book written by Marcus Vincentius late in the fifteenth century, a picture of which may be seen in Edward
Johnston's *Writing & Illuminating & Lettering*, plate xx. It
was with deepest satisfaction that I found the key to the magnificent page construction of this masterpiece of calligraphy
within my canon, and over more than forty years I have not
ceased to admire the book. The type area is half the height of

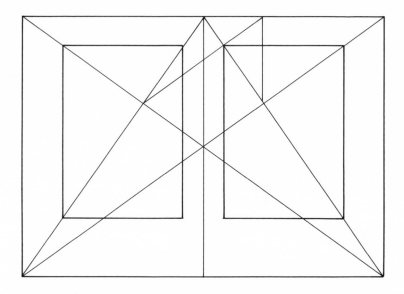

Figure 12. Page proportion 1: √2̄ (the D I N normal format).
Paper height and width divided into ninths.

the parchment, and the page (9.3 × 13.9 cm; 3⁵⁄₁₆ × 5½ in.) holds twelve lines of twenty-four letters each.

If necessary, the height of the paper may be divided any way you choose. Even narrower margins than those shown in figure 16 are possible, as long as the link between type area, single page diagonal and double page diagonal remains intact; only this guarantees a harmonious position of the type area.

The typographical system based on the number twelve, whose unit is the cicero or pica, divided into twelve points, has neither originally nor necessarily anything to do with the canon here related, not even with the book page of 2:3 proportion, which was the one used by both Gutenberg and Peter

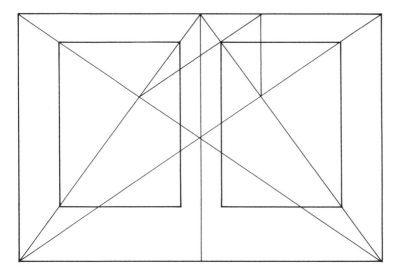

*Figure 13. Page proportion 3:4 (quarto). Paper height and width
divided into ninths. Here, too, the type area must mirror
the proportions of the page.*

Schöffer. When book printing began, the pica divided into
twelve parts was unknown and general rules did not exist.
Even the natural measurements taken from the human body,
like yard, foot and the width of a thumb, the inch, were not
defined exactly. It is likely that given lengths were divided using Villard's Diagram, and that every printer did his own calculations based on units that were not at all universally valid.

The convenience of determining all measurements, including the paper size, in picas and points for a page proportion of 2:3 is purely accidental. Other proportions are not so
obliging. If you have to work with proportions at all, a slide
rule or wheel is a necessity. From 1947 until 1949 I worked in
London, England, in order to completely rebuild the look of

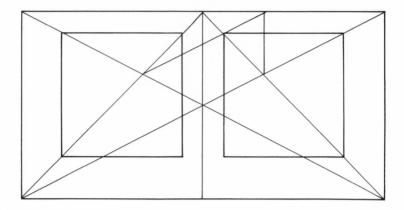

*Figure 14. Page proportion 1:1. Paper height and
width divided into ninths.*

all editions published by Penguin Books. I constantly had to
work in picas and to alternate between inch and centimetre.
Example: determine a proportional ratio in inches and
eighths-of-an-inch, find the equivalent value in centimetres
and millimetres, then check the numbers on a circular slide
rule. England neither reckons nor measures in the decimal
system, hence a tool like the slide rule is practically unknown
in the British book trade. Consequently an irrational relationship like the Golden Section has to be found by strictly
geometrical means (using compass and ruler). It doesn't hurt
to learn how to do this. But using a slide rule, I would set it at
1:1.618 or 21:34 and simply read that a book in the format
of the Golden Section, 18 centimetres high, has to be 11.1
centimetres wide.

Wherever possible the width of the type area should come
out even in full picas, or in half picas if absolutely necessary,
and the inner margin or gutter at least in half picas again. The
width of the trimmed top margin, and in fact the entire trim

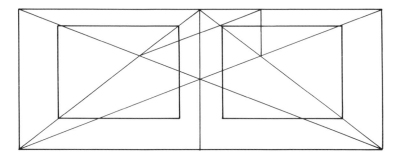

*Figure 15. Page proportion 4:3. Paper height and
width divided into ninths.*

size, has to be given in millimetres, even if all calculations
have been done in picas. A bookbinder knows millimetres
only. All of these specifications are contained in the pair of
specimen or sample pages, which must precede production.

Circumstances seldom permit the mathematically correct
size and positioning of a type area. Frequently we have to be
content with a close approximation of the ideal. Neither can
we always place the typographical text block as high as
would be desirable, nor, as a rule, is the calculated inner margin of sufficient width. Such a gutter will be correct only if the
book either consists of a single sheet only or lies perfectly flat
when opened. It is the *appearance* of the open book that has
to relate to the canon. The gutter must *appear* to be as wide as
the outer margins. Unfortunately it is not only shadow but
also the small portion of the paper that disappears in the sew-
ing or stitching that diminish the visible width of the gutter.

And there is no infallible formula that tells us how much
to add for binding. Much depends upon how this is done. As
a rule, fat books need a little more room than slender volumes. The weight of the paper counts for a little as well. If we

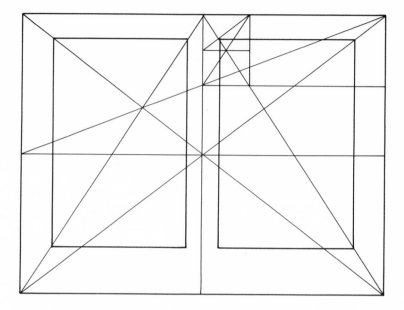

*Figure 16. Page proportion 2:3. Paper height and width divided
into twelfths, using Villard's Diagram, as shown in figure 9.
A geometrical division is simpler and better than an
arithmetical computation.*

want to be certain, we have to trim a pair of pages down to
the print area and then glue them into a dummy volume of the
finished book. This dummy must already include the prob-
able or likely addition for binding. Otherwise the outside
margins will not be correct. Perhaps the dummy may have to
be altered accordingly later, *i.e.* it may have to be widened or
trimmed down. An additional millimetre or two of trim
width in the sewn book hardly affects the proportions of the
cover or case, since book cases protrude approximately 2.5
mm at the face and 2 mm each at both head and foot; in all
they are 4 mm higher than the sewn book. Furthermore, it is

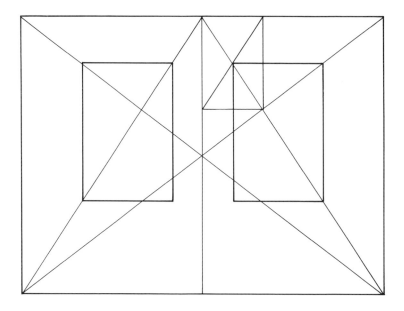

Figure 17. Page proportion 2:3. Page height and width divided into sixths. Both applied in a little prayer book written by Marcus Vincentinus (Marcus de Cribellariis) in the late fifteenth century.

the open book that counts, the exposed pages; the size of the case or cover is determined by the sewn and trimmed book and does not matter here.

Choice of type size and of leading contribute greatly to the beauty of a book. The lines should contain from eight to twelve words; more is a nuisance. The broader margins resulting from division by nine permit a slightly larger type size than does the division by twelve. Lines with more than twelve words require more leading. Typesetting without leading is a torture for the reader.

Nor is it fruitless to point out the correspondence between type width and page proportion. A square book format, not exactly one of the best, needs a broad type, so that the shapes of the letters o and n more closely coincide with the format of the book. Narrow type would be entirely unsuited to a square book. On the other hand, typefaces of the familiar format are correct for the usual shape of books since the contours of the letters o and n closely resemble the proportion of the page.

The page number does not belong to the text block. It stands alone. As a rule I use centered numerals at the foot of the type area. This is usually the best and also the simplest solution by far. In exceptional cases I will place my page numbers under the text block near the outside. As a rule I then draw them in by a quad so as not to cause discord with a partially blank last line of text.

Medieval manuscripts show small page or leaf numbers in the upper outer corner of the parchment.

It is better not to count a centered running head without a separating rule as part of the text block, especially when the page number is at the bottom. However, if there is a rule between text and running head, then both are part of the text block.

When typography hit bottom near the end of the nineteenth century, all manner of styles were copied naïvely in their obvious outward appearance, like initials and vignettes. Yet no one thought about page proportions. Painters attempted to free the shoddy typography from atrophied rules, and in doing so, they objected to everything that might infringe upon the newly declared artistic freedom. Subsequently they had small or no regard for exact proportions. They abhorred mention of the Golden Section, possibly because for a time people had abused the ancient proportion as

Figure 18.

A *1:2.236 (1: $\sqrt{5}$)*   E *3:5*   H *2:3*

B *1:2 (1: $\sqrt{4}$)*   F *1:1.618 (21:34)*   I *1:1.414 (1: $\sqrt{2}$)*

C *5:9*   *(Golden Section)*   K *3:4*

D *1:1.732 (1: $\sqrt{3}$)*   G *1:1.538 (Figure 1)*

a general recipe for producing *art,* dividing and shaping just about everything according to it. For this reason no one intentionally used book formats of rational or irrational proportions any more; nor did anyone care about a planned type area. If a beautiful book appeared now and again, it was because an exceptional person had cared enough to look at masterful works of the past, had abstracted a few rules, had developed a *feel* for good proportions between page size and text block position. Unfortunately, such an indefinable *feel* is neither a reliable rule, nor can it be taught. Real progress can be achieved only through tireless scientific study of the flawless works of the past. It is this unflagging effort in the meticulous investigation of old masterpieces that we have to thank for the most important printed works of the present; only research into the secrets of old book formats and type areas will in the end bring us much closer to the true art of making a book.

In the first half of our century one wanted to limit the great number of available raw sheet formats. The average side proportion of the old formats, 3:4, which gave us a quarto format of 3:4 and an octavo format of 2:3, was quite sensible. However, some people saw a disadvantage in the variety of proportions offered by quarto and octavo. Thus today's *normal* format was created based on the proportion of $1: \sqrt{2}$, which is retained when the sheet is folded. But the fact that no one paid much attention to page proportions is coming back to haunt us. This lack of attention led to the baby being tossed out with the bath water, as the large number of old formats was reduced to little more than one. Many people believe this narrow norm of paper formats to be the answer to all their format problems. This is an error. The selection among the new formats is much too small; the hybrid proportion of $1: \sqrt{2}$ is only one of many, and is certainly not always the best.

Figure 18 provides an overview of all rectangular proportions mentioned here and also gives the rare ratio of $1: \sqrt{5}$. A, D, F, G, and I are irrational relationships, while B, C, E, H and K are rational ones.

Anyone who produces books and other printed material must first look for suitable paper sheet sizes of the correct proportions. Even the most beautiful script does not help if the format, say A5, is unpleasant to start with. In the same way, a disharmonious text block in an unfortunate position destroys all potential beauty.

Countless type areas, even in the slender formats, are too high. Dissonant or unharmonious book pages cannot be avoided when our innate desire to see a text block proportioned according to the Golden Section, or at least approximating it, is confronted by a page format in $1: \sqrt{2}$ proportion or 3:4. If we want to create a harmonious page from one of the new sheet formats, we either have to alter the page format, or we have to set the text block in proportion with the page format. Nobody will gripe about good paper proportions as long as there are choices left to be made. The correct type area, the other condition for a beautiful book, has seldom been researched, still less in any methodical manner. Like typography itself, in the nineteenth century, the type area was neglected to such a degree that any alteration seemed permissible. The recent history of the text block is full of attempts to push aside old and unsatisfactory results and replace them with the unconventional.

What all these attempts have in common is arbitrariness. The old law had been lost, and it was not to be found again with ‹feeling› alone. This is where I succeeded by measuring countless medieval manuscripts. The rediscovered canon, shared here, is free from all arbitrariness and ends all laborious groping. In all its many variations it will inevitably lead to books where page format and text block agree with one another and become a harmonious unit.

LITERARY REFERENCES IN CHRONOLOGICAL ORDER

GUSTAV MILCHSACK. Kunst-Typographie (Art-Typography). In: *Archiv für Buchgewerbe.* Vol. 8: 291–295; Vol. 10: 365–372. Lepzig, 1901. The attempt of a knowledgeable bibliophile to track down the laws of beauty in the proportions of old books. He believes that he can express page proportions in rational numbers.

EDWARD JOHNSTON. *Manuscript Inscription Letters.* Second edition. London: John Hogg, 1911. Plate 1: Empirical determination of page proportions in numbers; incontestable in the only example shown.

EDWARD JOHNSTON. *Writing & Illuminating & Lettering.* Seventh edition. London: John Hogg, 1915. Pages 103–7; plate XX. Theory of page proportions based on practical experience. Only numerical proportions given.

FRIEDRICH BAUER. *Das Buch als Werk des Buchdruckers* (The Book as a work of the Printer). Leipzig: Deutscher Buchgewerbe Verein, 1920. The work of a knowledgeable person. On the whole still valid today. Influenced by Milchsack and others, he believes in rational page proportions.

E. W. TIEFENBACH. *Über den Satz im schönen Buch* (About typesetting in beautiful books). Berlin: Officina Serpentis, 1930. One of the most important sentences in this confession is cast merely as an aside: ‹ To arrive at the proportions of a page, one is somewhat dependent upon the dimensions of the printing paper and its proportions. › Not exactly perfect grammar, and a pity indeed that he doesn't follow up on this basically correct thought.

JAN TSCHICHOLD. Die Maßverhältnisse der Buchseite, des Schriftfeldes und der Ränder (The proportions of book page, type area and margins). In: *Schweizer Graphische Mitteilungen* 65, 294–305. St Gallen, August 1946. An early attempt by the author. Contains more examples than theories. Many illustrations.

JOH. A. VAN DE GRAAF. Nieuwe berekening voor de vormgeving (A new way to compute form). In: *Tété*, 1946: 95–100. Amsterdam, November 1946. Shows the simplest way to divide paper height and width into ninths.

HANS KAYSER. *Ein harmonikaler Teilungskanon* (A canon for harmonious page division). Zürich: Occident-Verlag, 1946. Brilliant and deep, like all books by this author. Makes reference to Villard de Honnecourt's canon, which is hidden in his workshop record book.

JAN TSCHICHOLD. Die Proportionen des Buches (The proportions of a book). In: *Der Druckspiegel* 10: 8–18, 87–96, 145–150. Stuttgart: January, February, March, 1955. Written in 1953. The first publication by the author of his determination of the late medieval manuscript canon. Numerous diagrams and illustrations. Superseded in part by the present collection.

JAN TSCHICHOLD. *Bokens Proportioner.* (The preceding essay in book form and in Swedish.) Göteborg: Wezäta, 1955. A beautifully printed edition.

JAN TSCHICHOLD. *De proporties van de boek.* (The same work, in Dutch.) Amsterdam: Intergrafia, 1955.

WOLFGANG VON WERSIN. *Das Buch vom Rechteck* (The book of the rectangle). Ravensburg: Otto Maier, 1956. An interpretation of the properties of the more important rectangles and their role in architecture. Does not deal with books.

RAÚL M. ROSARIVO. *Divina proporción typográfica.* La Plata, 1956. Published in German translation in 1961. Supports Tschichold's find of the late medieval manuscript canon, figure 5. Errs in the evident opinion that a page proportion of 2:3, and this proportion alone, is the perfect one.

Typography and
the Traditional Title Page

A TITLE PAGE in its typographic form is an integral part of the book and as such has to match the typography of the other components.

Many book titles lack this convincing affinity with the following book pages. Even if the page setting is flawless, the book as a whole is a disappointment when, typographically speaking, the title has a displeasing and ungraceful effect. Frugality in ways and means must not become weakness or poverty. The titles of many books look as if they had been set at the very last minute, as if they had been declared ready for printing without any improvement, or as if someone had ordered the work, or done it himself, without the slightest care and attention. These title pages are like poorly dressed, anemic and fearful orphans. The art of traditional centered typography seems lost. A title, the herald of the text, has to be strong and healthy. It should not whisper. But, alas, healthy looking title pages are the exception. And really beautiful, unmistakable title pages are as rare as perfection itself.

An important prerequisite is good wording. ‹Matthias Grünewald ‖ The Altar of Isenheim › would be an erroneous and unusable formulation. ‹ The ‖ Altar of Isenheim ‖ by Matthias Grünewald › would be correct. The wording ‹Eduard Mörike ‖ Collected Works › is also disputable. Correct would be ‹ Mörike's ‖ Collected Works ›. Completely unbearable,

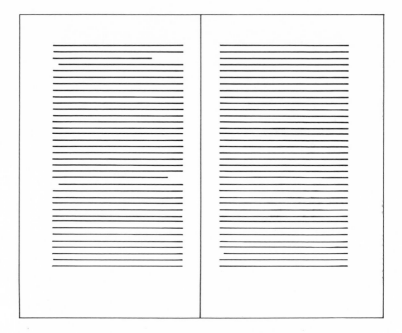

Figure 1. A pair of pages, schematic, for comparison with the erroneous position of the title in figure 2. Horizontally, a title must not move from the middle of the type area.

because of the bad grammar: ‹Collected Works by Eduard Mörike›. The genuine title ‹Eduard Mörike ‖ Maler Nolten›, however, can go the other way around: ‹Maler Nolten ‖ by Eduard Mörike›. One has to distinguish carefully between the original author's title and one freely fashioned by the publisher. A poorly or erroneously worded title impedes the creation of a good title page enormously.

Without an exact set of specimen or sample pages at hand it is not possible to develop a title properly or to judge the quality of its form.

A healthy title page can only be developed starting with

Figure 2. If the book margins are ample, then upper and lower margins are correct in this case. However, the title, as indicated, occupies the center of the page width, which is an error.

the book page. And the rules for margin proportions and positioning of the type area or text block apply equally to the title (figure 1). *The title must not,* as happens so frequently, *be placed in the center of the paper width* (figure 2). This would cause it to step outside the whole of the book. Nowhere must the lines of the title transgress beyond the limits allotted to the text block. As a rule it is almost always better to keep the major line of a title noticeably narrower than the full width of the set. Nor should titles reach up to the total height of a page, in particular when the page has very narrow margins.

Even a short title should ‹fill› a book page. This means that it should possess proper substance. Frequently, however, one seems to fear using larger type sizes. The major line of a title should be at least two sizes larger than the basic type of the book. There are no fixed rules in this matter because to set a title is a job where an educated sensitivity to form has to culminate in a decision. Even short titles set in relatively small letter sizes can ‹fill› a page if the arrangemment is a clever one. Perhaps it is possible to break a long major line. The resulting two shorter lines in the important upper group on the title page will now have a more polyhedral contour instead of a linear shape. The enormous white expanse between the title cluster and the publisher's imprint must not appear accidental and ‹empty›. The tension of this white space must contribute to the effect of the whole. A good publisher's emblem could be useful, but it isn't absolutely necessary. If one is being used, it has to blend in smoothly with the typography, and its thickest lines must not be thicker than the thickest lines of the largest type used in the title, nor should its thinnest lines be finer than the thinnest lines of the smallest type used. Black publisher's signets with negative letters constitute ugly intruders within the overall structure of a title page (figure 9). Not only are they strangers in the land of book typography, but they endanger the book page itself since they shine through to the other side. A publisher's emblem should be light, to match the type color. A good emblem is a work of art. It doesn't have to be really small since squeamishness and timidity ill become a title page. Not every graphic artist can draw a useable publisher's emblem, however. The develop-

Right: Figure 3. French book title of 1510. The kind of line breaks shown here are taboo today.

68

Les lunettes des prin
ces auec aultũes balades et additi-
ous nouuellemẽt cõposees p noble
hõe Jehã meschinot Escuier/en sõ
biuant grant maistre dhostel de la
Royne de France.

ment of an emblem is not simple and usually runs through a number of expensive stages.

If an emblem is not wanted on the title page, it could be used for a half-title. During the Art Nouveau period, a tendency developed to place the emblem in the upper right-hand corner of the print area on the half-title page, a position where the Insel Verlag kept its logo for years. Today such a position would appear too deliberate. It is probably better to place the signet on page 3 in the optical center of the paper height and the middle of the text block width (pages 1 and 2 should be left unprinted, like the last two pages of the book). The best place, it seems to me, would be the page with printer's information: the colophon at the end of the book, if one should elect, against common usage, to put it there.

Printers of the Gothic, the Renaissance and the Baroque had it fairly easy creating good title pages. Either the publisher's emblem or another large, illustrative woodcut formed the center of the title page and adequately opened up the book (figures 3 and 4). During the eighteenth century this decoration gave way to a somewhat smaller vignette, either a woodcut again or a copper engraving (figure 5). Today titles with publishers' emblems are more of an exception. What has remained is the empty, unused space between the title cluster near the top and the publisher's imprint near the bottom of the page (figures 8 and 17).

One of the difficulties in setting a good title is the contour, the typographical outline of the title cluster, which is partly determined by any break in the wording and partly by the gradation of type sizes; both have to go hand in hand with

Right: Figure 4. Beautiful book title from the French Renaissance, Paris, 1585. Note the large publisher's emblem.

LES

ODES D'ANACREON

TEIEN, POETE GREC,

traduictes en François,

PAR REMY BELLEAV.

Auec quelques petites Hymnes de son in-
uention, & autres diuerses poësies:
Ensemble vne Comedie.

TOME SECOND.

A PARIS,

Pour Gilles Gilles, Libraire, rue S. Iehan
de Latran, aux trois Couronnes.

M. D. LXXXV.

logic and the value of the individual word within the sequence. Many of the demands placed upon today's title pages are leftovers from the rationalism of the eighteenth and nineteenth centuries. Unlike the printers of the Gothic, Renaissance and Baroque (figures 3 and 4), we are not permitted to break words and lines wherever the outward typographical appearance makes this desirable; nor are we permitted to choose type sizes without regard for the sense of the phrase. Instead, we have to adhere strictly to the meaning of the word. Nor is it simple, without the use of an emblem, to achieve a degree of balance between the often heavy major title cluster near the top and the usually less extensive publisher's imprint near the bottom. This is why it is more difficult today to set a good title page, especially in roman, than it was in the sixteenth and seventeenth centuries.

The body of a drinking vessel provides one of the most useful contours for the shape of a title (figures 10 and 14), if it can be achieved without apparent effort. The stem of the glass, in this case, is replaced by the publisher's emblem. But this is extremely rare. Our titles are too short for this. We should be content if we succeed in achieving a pleasant outline and a good balance between the two major clusters of words.

One thing in particular is necessary: both clusters, the upper and the lower, have to appear as planes instead of lines, and wherever possible should contain several lines (figure 2); if necessary they may be broken and haltered for the purpose. German words, frequently long, don't make it exactly easy to obtain a good outline, especially if we have to use roman or,

Right: Figure 5. French title page by Barbou, 1759, showing woodcut emblem (a print shop).

MARCI ACCII

PLAUTI

COMŒDIÆ

QUÆ SUPERSUNT

TOMUS I.

META LABORIS HONOS

PARISIIS,

Typis J. BARBOU, viâ San-Jacobæâ, ſub
Signo Ciconiarum.

M. DCC. LIX.

worse yet, roman capitals. Perhaps also, roman capitals are used too frequently and lowercase roman not often enough. Fraktur results in significantly shorter and hence more poly-gonal and stronger word images. As a consequence, Fraktur gives better results than roman for the title pages of German books (figures 8 and 12). It is unfortunate that during Goethe's time typography as a whole was weak and unsure of itself. The patchy title pages of the day are hardly exemplary (see figure 6).

A proper title page has to be set from the same type family that has been used for the book – in Garamond, for example, when the book is set in Garamond, or in an ordinary old-style when such has been used for the book. Using Jannon's French Baroque type for the title page of a book otherwise set in an Italian humanist face creates displacement and disharmony. One can hardly overstate the case for strictness here. Semi-bold letters, even from the same family, should never be used for titles. There isn't the slightest reason to use them. Hand-lettered titles are thinkable; however, to letter them in such a manner that they really harmonize with text page and type-face is a subtle art indeed, and not something understood by every calligrapher. Even the best typography, difficult as it may be, is simpler to handle and, above all, more flexible.

The most important prerequisite for setting a good title page is a sensitive rapport with letters. From now on we shall think in terms of roman title pages only. When lines with cap-ital letters are being used, these must be spaced boldly and without hesitation, though with a care to retain balance. A single point is never enough between H and I. Instead, space

Right: Figure 6. German title page from the time of Goethe. Not a shining example. Roman imitated with Fraktur.

74

Torquato Tasso.

Ein Schauspiel.

Von

Goethe.

Aechte Ausgabe.

Leipzig,

bey Georg Joachim Göschen.

1790.

Chinefifche Lyrif

vom 12. Jahrhundert v. Chr. bis zur
Gegenwart

In deutscher Überfetzung, mit
Einleitung und Anmerkungen
von
Hans Heilmann

München und Leipzig
R. Piper & Co.

Chinefifche Lyrif

vom zwölften Jahrhundert vor Chriftus
bis zur Gegenwart
in deutscher Überfetzung,
mit Einleitung und Anmerkungen
von Hans Heilmann

1958
München und Frankfurt,
im Verlag Piper

*Left: Figure 7. Book title, approximately 1905. Not well designed.
Faulty detail work. Right: Figure 8. The same text, as one
would typeset it today, and better. Not letterspaced.*

the smallest sizes using 1½ points, and the larger ones, up to
12-point, using 2 to 2½ points. From 14 points on up, use
three or more points for letterspacing. Lines with unspaced
or poorly spaced caps are always ugly. The letters are glued
together, so to speak, and result in a mess of lines difficult to
decipher. Often the spacing is too weak. Consequently it happens that a letter may have to be filed to reduce a gap, say between V A, that seems too large. The procedure is a reprehensible one and entirely unnecessary if spacing is done boldly.
The space in V A should be used as the smallest optical dis-

76

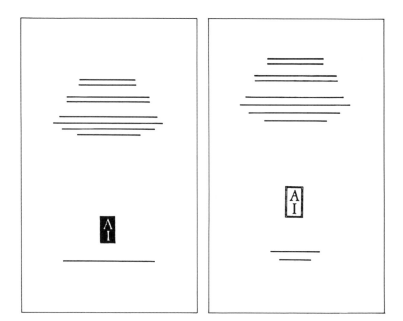

Left: Figure 9. A title page unfortunately typical of today, with the head in the abdominal region and the emblem in negative.
Right: Figure 10. The same title, corrected. The emblem is now positive.

tance. Even in LA there has to exist a small space, a spacelet, at the very least the thickness of a card.

Lowercase roman and italic letters in a title must never be spaced. It is an error to rationalize the spacing of lowercase letters on the same grounds that cause us to space uppercase letters.

Numbers as part of the title text (‹with 240 illustrations›) must be spelled out (‹with two-hundred-and-forty illustrations›, ‹eighteenth century›); only the year may be given in arabic numerals (1958). In works of particular merit – hardly in others though – the year may appear in roman numerals (M C M L V I I I), especially if the entire title has been set in uppercase roman.

The fewer type sizes in a title, the better! Many cooks spoil the broth, and too many sizes the title. To use four or five sizes is a difficult thing (figure 16). Only in exceptional cases is it necessary to use more than three sizes; now and again even two are sufficient (figures 8 and 11).

A title set in roman majuscules only, while it tends to look formal, almost always appears harmonious. This is no reason, however, to make this form the rule. Lowercase letters lend expression to major lines, while at the same time shorter lines may benefit from uppercase letters (figure 15).

Never is the publishing house more important than the author, and at most it should be set no larger than the author's name. How often do people deny this order of precedence and set the author's name even smaller than the publisher's designation! And, alas, it even happens that the name of the publisher is set as large as the major line of the upper cluster.

As we can see, the playing field of correct title setting is encumbered with many restrictions, warnings and prohibitions: the limits of the type area, little freedom in typeface selection, limited type sizes, no semibold letters, unconditional spacing of uppercase letters. With all this in mind, we may now attempt to work on setting a title page.

Right: Figure 11. A title page by the author. (Wood engraving by Reynolds Stone.) 1947. Overleaf, page 80: Figure 12. A title page by the author in the style of the German Rococo. 1957. Overleaf, page 81: Figure 13. A title page by the author, set in Monotype Bell. 1954.

78

WILLIAM SHAKESPEARE

THE SONNETS

AND

A LOVER'S COMPLAINT

PENGUIN BOOKS

HARMONDSWORTH · MIDDLESEX

ENGLAND

Schönste liebe mich

Deutsche Liebesgedichte
aus dem Barock und dem Rokoko

Mit farbigen Wiedergaben
acht alter Spitzenbildchen

Verlag Lambert Schneider,
Heidelberg

YORICKS

EMPFINDSAME

REISE

DURCH FRANKREICH UND ITALIEN

—

AUS DEM

ENGLISCHEN ÜBERSETZT VON

JOHANN JOACHIM BODE

—

BIRKHÄUSER VERLAG

BASEL

A good way to begin is this: using a black ballpoint or fountain pen – not a lead pencil – carefully sketch all words in the sizes you consider suitable, referring to type samples. A beginner in particular must be careful not to hand a doodle sketch to the typesetter. Instead, he should attempt to draw each letter as accurately as possible. Only the very experienced may work with seeming carelessness. Merely blocking out lines, as I have done in some of my illustrations, will mislead without fail! Next, the lines are cut and placed on an empty pair of pages made from the same paper and in the exact size of the book; on the right-hand side a thin pencil line indicates the limit of the text block. Now we move things around again and again, and we may perhaps want to change the size of the letters, until finally we think we have found the best possible solution. Now we paste the lines in place, using waterless glue (rubber cement). At the head of the sketch we indicate the typeface (say, ‹everything in Janson›), in the margin we indicate the exact type sizes (say, ‹10, lower-case›, ‹8, uppercase, spaced 1½ pt›); it is important to specify the precise spacing for uppercase letters. We also indicate ‹height exactly like type area› or ‹height and position according to sketch›, and finally we plead, ‹print in correct position according to sketch on trimmed double-page›. Now our sketch can go to the typesetter. If our drawing is competent and workmanlike and happens to end up in good hands, then we shall get back exactly what we labored to achieve and what should now have become a convincing unit. Frequently, however, the work is not executed according to the specifications: the leading has been altered, the spacing is no

Right: Figure 14. An imaginary title page, well set,
but it lacks originality.

DIE

FÜRSTIN VON CLEVE

VON

MARIE MADELEINE

GRÄFIN VON

LAFAYETTE

IM VERLAG ZUM EINHORN

ZU BASEL

longer balanced. Or one finds fault with the spacing of words, which more often than not is too wide. The great E. R. Weiss gave all his corrections in millimetres rather than in points; this example is not to be followed. Typesetters calculate in points, and how many points are there in half-a-millimetre? ‹½ pt.› is specific; ‹a touch more› could mean anything at all. Setting a title is partly the ‹art of the point›, indeed of the half-point. ‹Space this› is an unclear instruction. One has to indicate clearly ‹add ½ pt. spacing› or ‹space 1½ points›.

It can happen that the first proof is flawless in every respect. Yet, it may also happen that the proof looks somewhat different from what the designer had in mind, and he has to alter and correct matters here and there. Then new proofs have to be ordered in the right format and with correct positioning, until the title reaches home. The title sketches and indeed all of the title work should be enclosed with the text manuscript and the first page proofs of the title should arrive with the text galleys. The specification pages have to be examined and approved before the typesetter gets the go-ahead.

Even when it is narrower and lower than the book page, a good title in all its extensions has to follow the outline proportions of the page to some degree. Otherwise it doesn't suit the page. If the upper cluster of the title is narrow already, then the publisher's imprint may never claim the full width of the type area (figure 9). Frequently the major cluster is placed far too low (figure 9). The designers of these title pages seem to feel that the publisher's imprint does not partake of the overall shape. Such a title page looks droopy and sagging. After all, the publisher's imprint is just as visible as the upper

Right: Figure 15. The same title page, using unspaced lowercase letters in the major line. Much better than figure 14.

DIE

Fürstin von Cleve

VON

MARIE MADELEINE

GRÄFIN VON

LAFAYETTE

IM

VERLAG ZUM EINHORN

ZU BASEL

cluster, and together, as a whole, they have to sit right. One expects the major line within the upper third of a title page and not at the optical center! Titles as shown in figure 9 are defective. Further, the long and linear shape of the publisher's imprint ought to be changed (in the original it was set with lowercase letters, then ruined by spacing) because it contradicts the rounded form of the upper group. Here as everywhere, lines of equal length one beneath the other would be quite undesirable. Only when the upper cluster has been raised and the lower one turned into a double line and thus narrowed is the title seated properly (figure 10).

‹Appropriate› leading between the lines of type is easily requested yet a difficult thing to achieve. Not only must the spaces between the lines not contradict the content but, like the lines themselves, the leading has to contribute to the overall effect. Since the greater portion of a title page is usually unprinted, clusters of lines with little spacing appear alien; the white of the background has to penetrate. Large and wide margins simply demand healthy leading, even between lines of the same type size. A certain transparency of the title typography is usually desirable. Otherwise, typesetting and background are not compatible and cannot fuse into a single unit (figures 11, 12 and 13).

If, as is the case in pocketbooks, the margins are very narrow, then the title must not fill the type area. If it did, the upper cluster would sit far too high and would have to be lowered – and the publisher's imprint raised correspondingly! The proportional relationship between upper and lower margins of a book page has to show up in the title as well.

Right: Figure 16. Finally, this kind of typography captures the spirit of the time. But it isn't as simple as it looks.

DIE FÜRSTIN VON

CLEVE

VON

Marie Madeleine Gräfin
von Lafayette

Im Verlag zum Einhorn

BASEL

87

Further, the upper cluster frequently has to be lowered a little (and the publisher's imprint raised correspondingly) if the very first line is the major one. A shorter first line, especially when set in a type size smaller than the major line, while always welcome, cannot always be had. Besides, the author's name may be placed above the first line or, following it, be joined with the word *by*. There are occasions when the word *by* wants to occupy a line of its own. This strongly emphasizes the center axis of the page. At other times such a short line is not pleasing and *by* is placed in the author's line in front of the name.

On the reverse of the title page we usually find particulars, if not about the publisher, then about the edition and the printer (frequently, and erroneously, also about the designer of the jacket, which doesn't belong to the book proper. This may be present even if the design is not at all remarkable or, indeed, poor). For very inexpensive books there is no other solution since no space can be found at the end of the book. Yet there is no reason for careless typesetting here, even in the most inexpensive books. Select a very small size of the basic typeface (no spacing), look for a pleasing sequence of lines, and for leading use approximately the same number of points that was used for the text. Much more cultivated and composed are lightly spaced small caps of a small type size when the leading of the text is used. The wording should be as tight as possible. Since these lines will shine through the title page, they should be arranged so as to fall on groups or lines of the title itself and not extend beyond them, wherever possible.

Of late, these particulars on the back of a title page have

Figure 17. A title page by the author. A standard solution that can easily be modified.

VIRGINIA WOOLF

A Room of One's Own

PENGUIN BOOKS

HARMONDSWORTH · MIDDLESEX

grown in fearsome fashion, reminiscent of the almost endless list of credits before a film finally begins, and for the time being at least, they are as obtrusive as they are unwanted. The contributors, modestly, should call attention to themselves at the end of the book. To be cited by name at the beginning is the privilege solely of the author and of the book's midwife, the publisher. I have always been a heretic, and it is my opinion that all other particulars should be relegated to a place at the end of the book, after the text.

Since the first text page of a book should have an empty facing page, one could achieve this by placing the title, without author, facing the copyright page, much like a bastard title. This would leave the left-hand page facing the beginning of the text empty. Only in the least expensive of books should we find anything printed here, and if anything is, it should be presented neatly. Regrettably it is this page which is being treated with the least care, and it therefore shows the true competence of the book's designer. There are three reasons why we have not mentioned heretofore this grey eminence, the designer of the book. First, the publisher doesn't like it. Second, the designer of the book is too modest, even though he is surely more important than, say, the graphic artist who designed the jacket. And third, the designer himself doesn't want it, for the simple reason that, until the day of publication, he lives in fear of someone bungling the job. The author fears the typesetter, the printer fears the binder, and the designer is afraid of all four. He feels responsible. Yet, in spite of eagle eyes and the greatest circumspection, like the bodyguard of a dictator, he knows that mistakes will happen. He's

*Left: Figure 18. Colophon at the end of the book
shown in figure 12.*

Die Originale
der abgebildeten acht Spitzenbilder gehören
Jan Tschichold in Basel,
der auch die Zusammenstellung der Gedichte,
die Typographie und den Entwurf
zum Einbande dieses Buches
besorgt hat.
Die typographischen Zieraten sind
einem Straßburger Druck aus dem Jahre 1764
entnommen.
Satz und Druck der Buchdruckerei
H. Laupp jr, Tübingen.
Fünffarbenätzungen und Druck der Abbildungen:
Graphische Kunstanstalten F. Bruckmann KG,
München.
Werkdruckpapier von
Robert Horne & Co. Ltd, London.
Kunstdruckpapier von der
Papierfabrik Scheufelen, Oberlenningen.
Buchbinderarbeiten
von Willy Pingel, Heidelberg.
Erstes bis sechstes Tausend.
1957

been there. So he leaves both fame and shame to the pedestrians who, in naïve self-love, line themselves up on the page of particulars and wish to be noticed even before a single line of text has been read.

On the other hand, the reader doesn't care in the least who printed the book and whatever else may be related in the way of earth-shaking details on the back of the title page. All this information about the printer, the edition, even the names of the editor and that of the translator are best left for the end of the book (figure 18).

The two very last pages of a well-made book, like the two first ones, should be left entirely unprinted; *this also applies to volumes with reproductions of artworks at the end.* The third- or fourth-last page of the book is the best place for notes about the editor, the printer and so on (figure 18), and here the year of publication should be mentioned as well if it has been withheld from the title page.

And now back to the title. Figure 14 shows the flawless title of an imaginary book. The basic type is Jannon's, *i.e.* ‹Garamond›. Because a title is typographically flawless does not imply that it is a good, a perfect title. This title, and ‹Garamond› as the basic typeface, would be right if we had some kind of novel on our hands. But this novel is different. Written in 1678, it is the earliest European novel we have and, like the very first Japanese novel, *Genji,* 670 years older, it is the work of a woman. The book requires a certain typographical atmosphere and should be set in the Kis (‹Janson›) roman or, almost better yet, a Fraktur of Luther's time. Figure 15 shows the first attempt at a ‹Janson› title page for the book.

Figure 19. Title page by the author, 1945. Set in Caslon.
Monochrome decoration.

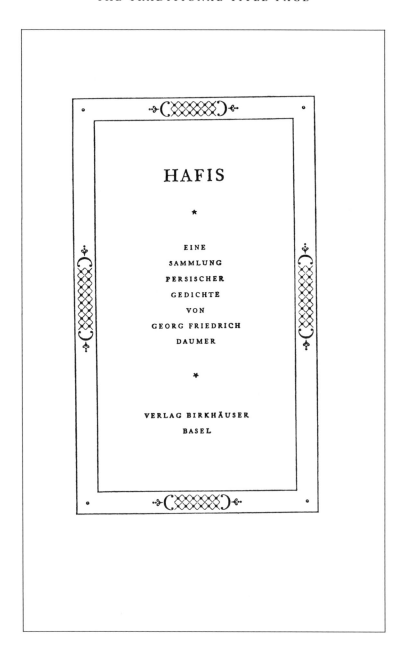

HAFIS

★

EINE
SAMMLUNG
PERSISCHER
GEDICHTE
VON
GEORG FRIEDRICH
DAUMER

★

VERLAG BIRKHÄUSER
BASEL

Better, but the mood of the times has not yet been fully captured, and figure 16 is just beginning to approach a good solution. We are not dealing here with the historicism of the 1880s but are attempting to fuse the style of the time around 1678 with the legitimate expectations of form of today. Searching after trendiness is infantile. Books are not articles of fashion. A title page for this book ‹in the spirit of the present›, a time of ergonomic steel furniture, aerodynamic car bodies and orbital satellites, could only be the monstrous product of an uneducated fool. Figure 12 shows the final solution of a similar task, a typographic interpretation of the mood of the work.

Usually, however, we are already satisfied if a title does not offend the mind and the eye, if it is in keeping with the basic requirements, as demonstrated, for good, harmonious and healthy form, and especially if it sits properly on the page. *Videant sequentes.*

House Rules for Typesetting:
the Publisher's Standing Instructions
for the Typesetter

COMMUNICATION between publisher and typesetter can be difficult at times if the typesetter still works to rules that do not meet the requirements of good typesetting. It is the quality of the setting that determines the appearance of the book. Even if the text face should not be particularly beautiful, a good effect can be achieved if good practices are being followed. On the other hand, even the most beautiful text letter will be despoiled if the spacing is too loose and if no attention is paid to the finer points of good typesetting. The following guidelines ensure a faultless text block. A publisher will not be disappointed if he obliges his typesetters to follow them.

Not covered are questions of leading, of page height, of the ratio between text-block width and type area in relation to the paper format. The complex nature of these matters does not permit setting them down in the form of short guidelines. They are covered elsewhere in this book.

Guidelines

Three-to-em spacing must be used in all headings and especially in setting text. Care must be taken to make the spaces between the words in a line optically equal, in particular when type is being handset.

After the *period* at the end of a sentence or abbreviation, the space should be the *normal* one used between the words of the line. Only in widely spaced lines is it permitted to leave a larger gap, and in this case, commas and hyphens should be treated in the same way. Between word and parentheses there must be spaces, except before A, J, T, V, W, Y, after a period, and in tightly spaced lines.

Commas and periods following single letters and abbreviations, such as *i.e.,* etc., or C.F. Meyer, require *reduced* spacing.

Headings and title clusters must be set without a period at the end.

Lowercase letters must never be spaced out. Instead of spacing, italic is to be used.

Uppercase letters are to be spaced with great care (for sizes above 8-point, use at least 1½ points). It is better to keep them a little wide instead of too tight.

Always use an *em-quad* for indention. Larger indents, which are neither more prominent nor more beautiful, should only be used if the lines are excessively long. If the indention is too large it may happen that the exit line is shorter than the indent following.

The *em dash* should be used only in tabular matter such as price tables. In all other cases use shorter dashes (en dashes). The hyphen must not replace a dash.

When setting in roman, *single guillemets* ‹ ›, or French quotation marks should be used as a rule. These must retain the same shape throughout the work. Except in tightly set lines they must be separated from the word by small spaces. Only quotations within a quotation require double guillemets: « ».

Superscript numbers must be set in the character of the basic font. Neither in the text nor in the footnote itself should the numeral or the asterisk be enclosed in parentheses. Between word and following superscript there should be a small space.

Footnotes are separated from the text block either by a space, never smaller than the general line spacing of the text area, or by a thin rule.

Umlauted capitals such as Ä, Ö, Ü must not be replaced by Ae, Oe, Ue (Ärzte, Äschenvorstadt).

In *numerals* the comma alone should be used to mark decimal places. Groups of one thousand must be spaced using small spaces instead of false commas or periods. 300,000 means three hundred, not three hundred thousand.* Three hundred thousand is to be set as 300 000. Periods must not be used to separate groups of a thousand. A comma always indicates a decimal place: 3,45 m; 420,500 kg. *Time,* however, is different. It is 2.30 A.M. Setting *telephone numbers,* it is better to separate the groups with small spaces rather than with a period: 328 171.

* *Tschichold's rule on commas and numerals is, of course, in line with standard European practice. But even in this book we have followed North American conventions instead.* – R B

97

What a Specimen Page
Should Look Like

WHEN a publisher plans a book, he wants to see proofs from his typesetter. Once these have been approved, after a little back-and-forth, they serve as obligatory prototypes for type-setter and printer.

Therefore it is necessary to prepare the specimen pages with the utmost care. For example, the height of the page must be perfectly clear. If two sizes of type are to be used, then one page must be set completely in the dominant size to determine the exact height of the type area. There must be no subtitles on this page. And in any case a pair of pages, a spread, should be presented. Not only will this reveal the over-all effect of the book, it also presents the only opportunity to show the beginning of a chapter. This is important for both the handsetter and the keyboard operator. It is best to place the beginning of the chapter on the left and the ordinary text page on the right. A book that is very complex typographi-cally may require three, four or even seven specimen pages because every capricious typesetting quirk must be seen.

Only after the typesetter has prepared the specimen pages can the work be calculated. Otherwise, the volume may be at variance with the plan. The overall conception cannot be left to theoretical procedures in the office. ‹Typesetting was cal-culated beforehand› is no excuse for an ugly book.

Setting the proofs cannot be done with any less care than

MAKE-UP SHEET
2nd proposal – 2 September 1965

Book: *Gottfried Keller, Der grüne Heinrich*
Publisher: Zum Venedig, Basel
Printer: Jakob Schnellhase, Basel

———

Page size, trimmed: 17.3 cm by 10 cm; 6⅞ in. by 4 in.
Basic font: Monotype Centaur 252, 10 on 11, 18 ciceros, 31 lines
Inside margin per page: 2 ciceros
Top margin, trimmed: 2 ciceros
Ä, Ö, ö, B, ‹ ›. En-dashes! Italics instead of spacing. Word spacing after periods (full stops).
Estimated volume: 576 pages (including 8 pages for bastard title (= page 1), title and foreword, plus 2 pages for table of contents at the end of the book. New chapters to be appended.

---

is given a normal job. When typographical errors show up even in the proofs, the printer will lose confidence in the proofreader. If the publisher requires his own guidelines to be used, then these have to be followed to the letter and the most important points must be outlined on the first page. (See the facing page.)

If the work contains footnotes, a detailed and complex example should be given.

Trimmed format, inner margin and head margin must be

absolutely exact. It has to be the ambition of a good printer to deliver immaculate proofs to the publisher.

In particular the paper, if it is available, should be the same as that of the edition being planned. If the actual paper is not yet on hand, the paper for the proofs should at least have a surface texture which closely resembles the final product.

Moreover, the printing itself must be first-class – no skimping on preparation and make-ready, and the ink intensity must be adjusted to suit paper and font. The pages should appear neither too dark nor too pale. It is these proofs which the printing foreman will use for a guide later.

Frequently the printer delivers only a single pitiful page, perhaps even with a short exit line at the foot to disfigure the lower margin. Real proofs consist of more than the minimal couple of pages; the particulars set out on the preceding page should appear in print on page one of a proper four-page proof. With this in hand, everything should be clear for the typesetter, the printing foreman and especially for the casual employees and workers involved.

Specimen pages of 10.9 × 17.25 cm instead of 11.0 × 17.3 cm could raise doubt whether the *real* size isn't 10.9 × 17.25 cm. Also, for every new try the volume has to be calculated anew. It isn't always the first try to which the publisher agrees. All attempts should be numbered and dated consecutively.

Further, it is advisable to fix permanently the widths of gutter and head margins on the specimen pages in order to avoid a mishap later.

A printer should make a sufficient number of proofs. At least four will go to the client, and the next four are retained for his own portfolio.

Only when all these guidelines are being followed carefully is there a reasonable chance that the finished book will satisfy the client as well as all those involved in its production.

Consequences of Tight Typesetting

TIGHT typesetting, usually and not quite correctly referred to as three-space or three-to-em setting, leads of necessity to a revision of typesetting rules that were formulated in the nineteenth century and that are still adhered to out of habit. Many of these older rules clash with three-space setting to such a degree that a decision will have to be made; accommodation between the two is not possible.

The reasons for tight typsetting are based on the optical experience that the older en quad (half em) spacing tends to tear the words of a sentence apart and make comprehension difficult. It results in a page image that is agitated, nervous, flecked with snow. Words in a line are frequently closer to their upper and lower neighbors than to those at the left and right. They lose their significant optical association.

Gutenberg's spacing and that prevailing in the fifteenth and sixteenth centuries was even tighter than that demanded today. It was thinner than the width of an i and we could almost call it four-to-em spacing. To be sure, a typesetter in those days had – and took – the opportunity to abbreviate words at will. Here is the reason why some of the incunabula, as well as Italian and French books of the sixteenth century, show a text block of inimitable perfection.

The ideal language for roman type is Latin, for which it was created. German texts contain long words and in the current orthography show accumulations of uppercase letters that are almost baroque; consequently, it is far more difficult to set a German text than an English one. Of all living languages, English gives the smoothest typographical image. English needs few uppercase letters and no accents at all, and the words are short.

As for the romance languages today, they are no longer as easy to set as their Latin mother. They use accents, and letters like z, j, and k, which are basically alien to roman. On the other hand, they remind one of Latin and do not carry the heavy burden of countless uppercase letters, as German does.

More than in other languages the long words in a German sentence make it necessary to divide words. While it is still possible to achieve a good and tight set in French and English works, word divisions and all, and even using the division rules of the nineteenth century, German requires a different treatment. Tight typesetting in German requires that the rules be relaxed and those about so-called ‹faulty division› be abolished altogether. *It is impossible to produce a tight set and avoid faulty divisions at the same time.* The result would be a mixture of lines that are tight, not so tight, and downright wide. Nor, if the set is to be tight and smooth, is it always easy to follow another German rule, not to divide at the end of a line three times in a row.

Tight typesetting requires that the spacing after a period be equal to, or under certain circumstances even narrower than, that between words. The older rules about the enlarged spacing (frequently like a white hole) at the end of a sentence should finally be done away with. It also makes life easier for the machine typesetter if periods require no special attention.

Tight typesetting affects page make-up as well. The rule that an exit line or widow must not begin a new page is not always acceptable with tight typesetting. True, these lines are not beautiful; but how to avoid them when nothing can be brought in or kicked out? (Compare also pages 135–137.)

As things stand, a first line at the bottom of a page – a widow – is not considered a mistake. It would be stretching matters to demand that those lines disappear. In most cases it would require the author to help with augmentations and eliminations. And this would mean establishing dominance of form over content, something a good typesetter must neither encourage nor demand.

Why the Beginnings of Paragraphs Must be Indented

WHEN WRITING down a sequence of thoughts, the author arranges them in the form of sentences which are grouped together. These groups of sentences are followed by a pause, a break. Today's unattractive section symbol § is no more than a poor variant of the medieval symbol ¶ which originally could also appear in the middle of running lines and was colored. It signified the beginning of a new group of sentences. During the late Middle Ages such groups of sentences were introduced with a new line, but the habit remained of beginning the new group with the symbol for paragraph, usually written in red. Some of the early printers even cut it as a type sort and printed it in black. Previously, though, it was inserted by hand in red by the *rubricator* (whose job description stems from the color: *rubrum* = red). The space for the symbol had to be left blank by the typesetter. But rubrication often did not take place, and it was found that the em quad indention or indent, as we call this empty space today, was sufficient by itself to define a new group of sentences, even without the red symbol.

This is still the case today. So far, no device more economical or even equally good has been found to designate a new group of sentences. There has been no shortage of attempts, though, to replace an old habit with a new one. But to destroy something old and replace it with something new, hoping that it will take hold, only makes sense if, first, there is a need to do this and, second, the new device is better than the old one.

This cannot be said of typesetting without indentions, though the new habit is spreading. It has a history also, albeit a short one. The desire of our time for simplicity is a reaction to the florid and ornate style of our grandfathers, frequently expressed in a morbid search after simplification. Such a confusion of ideas can have grave consequences. Around the turn of the century a few of the English printers discontinued indention, an ill-considered mannerism that in England has found few imitators to this day. Young publishers in Germany snapped it up, however. A very respected publisher, once operating in Leipzig, had many of his books set without indentions, contributing considerably to the spread of this dubious practice. If there were absolutely no other way, it might even be made to work, provided that reader, proofreader and typesetter try their very best to give the preceding line some form of exit (more generous than two or three typographical points!). However, in the second-rate columnar typesetting of newspapers, magazines and bookish printed material, this kind of typesetting, which is by no means cheaper than using em-quad indentions, becomes downright dangerous.

In newspaper work it is usual to place two or more points of leading between paragraphs, partly because newspapers do not have time for the careful make-ready of books. This practice is not exemplary, however.

The typesetter of a newspaper simply doesn't have the time to see to it that every last line of a column has a visible exit, *i.e.* a blank and empty space at the end. At times it happens that a line near the middle of a paragraph ends with a distinct period. The make-up man looks at these periods, and he adds additional leading, which then takes over the role of an indention. Has he made a mistake? There is no time for him to read the set. Nor does it worry the proofreader, reading hastily, primed to spot typographical errors. Time pressures him as well. As a result we get groups of sentences that have been cut erroneously and pasted without regard to sense. Further, the irregular and erratic leading spoils the look of a block of text. Of course, all this is plain and evident only to the serious reader.

Moreover, even when typesetter, reader and proofreader of a book without indentions try their very best to force artificial exits in lines preceding a new paragraph, not even as a team are they so infallible that these artificial and indirect indications will not somewhere be forgotten.

A book is printed for the reader, who at the end of a line is a little more sluggish than at the beginning. ‹Blunt› paragraph openings tend to create in him the impression that everything on the page is connected in a sensible manner, that he is reading a single paragraph. Yet a good writer chooses his paragraph breaks with great forethought and wants them to be recognizable as such. Typesetting without indention makes it difficult for the reader to comprehend what has been printed. And that is its most important disadvantage. While blunt beginnings seem to create a uniform and consistent impression when compared with normal typesetting, this impression is paid for with a serious loss of comprehension. And comprehension is definitely necessary if we want to think of a book as an ideal way to present a sequence of thoughts. Comprehension has to begin on the left, at the start of a line, and not at the end, where we stop reading. How troublesome that a matter so perfectly obvious still has to be explained!

There is only one place where an indention is an eyesore and doesn't make sense: under a *centered* heading. The first paragraph should begin bluntly. A heading that has been moved to the left requires an indention of the section following.

In passing, I will mention two more unsatisfactory methods of indirectly marking a paragraph: typesetting without indentions where the sections are separated by blank lines, which cause flagrant interruptions and at times leave the reader in doubt whether the new page indeed begins with a new paragraph; and exit lines that have been set flush right, an irritating nuisance and once again only a roundabout way of doing things.

There is indeed only one definite method, technically without flaw yet very simple and economical, to mark the beginning of a paragraph, and that is the indention. As a rule it is one em, the square of the type size (*i.e.* 10 points in a 10-point font), but there may be exceptions, and it could be made a touch smaller or, under certain circumstances, even a little larger. A typesetter is not likely to forget an indention. A proofreader is sure to notice it, and no reader will miss it. It is simply not true that typesetting with quad indents is less beautiful. Setting without indentions merely looks simpler, and it pays dearly for this through loss of comprehension, which is one attribute of typographical beauty. The fact that we see flush-left paragraph openings so frequently today does not demonstrate conclusively that they are good.

Of late, many literary works and scientific books as well have been set without indentions. A trend that started around the turn of the century has almost become a rule. People don't seem to notice the lack of intelligibility caused by this inarticulate presentation. This is an indication of the fading respect for word and letter. One editor of a special-interest magazine even thought that typesetting *with* indentions was something new and still had to prove its usefulness. He had it the wrong way around. It is typesetting *with* indentions that has proved itself for more than four hundred years. Only in Germany and Switzerland does one find frequent deviations from this practice. In England, France, the Scandinavian countries and the United States the ‹stammering› of flush-left paragraphs is a rare exception, used mainly in printed matter produced without care.

Normal, old-fashioned setting with indents is infinitely better and more intelligible than a smooth and natty set with blunt beginnings. It simply is not possible to improve upon the old method. It was probably an accidental discovery, but it presents the ideal solution to the problem. One may hope that the publishers and typesetters whose business it is will soon find their way back to this old solution.

A small portion of blame for spreading the flush-left habit must be shared also by typists. In writing letters and manuscripts on a typewriter, flush-left paragraphs are common, instead of the definite and always recognizable indent, and blank lines are used to separate paragraphs. Business schools – utterly incompetent when it comes to questions of typography – teach that indentions are old-fashioned and blunt beginnings are ‹modern›. This is an erroneous, unprofessional opinion. It would be a good thing if business schools returned to the old way. An indent of three or four letters is quite sufficient.

Italics, Small Capitals
and Quotation Marks in Books
and Scientific Publications*

A Little History

The beginning of typographical differentiation goes back to the Baroque. Here we find italic used within roman text as a means of differentiation. Books in German, set without exception in blackletter at the time, followed the fashion of distinguishing alien words by setting them in roman. The root syllables of alien words with German endings were set in roman and the endings themselves in Fraktur.

By the eighteenth century a few fixed rules had evolved for this kind of mixed typesetting, especially for scientific books. There were, and are, always publications whose text will benefit and become more lucid and comprehensive if some manner of type differentiation is applied. We cannot help but envy Immanuel Scheller's setting of the *Ausführliche lateinische Sprachlehre* (Comprehensive Latin Grammar), Leipzig, 1782 (see illustration). The basic font of this book is the Fraktur of the time. Translations into German were set in Schwabacher. J. F. Unger (1753–1840) used this beautiful, robust script in semibold. (Genuine semibold Fraktur scripts appeared in the nineteenth century.) But in Unger's opinion,

---

* Several scattered paragraphs and one entire section devoted to bibliographical style have been omitted from the translation of this essay. The excised passages focus exclusively on typographic practice in Germany, and it seemed pointless to repeat them in a language other than German. – R B

II) In allgemeinen Sätzen, die sich im Deutschen mit Man anfangen, als man sagt, glaubt, ist ꝛc. wird 1) die dritte Personalendung *numeri pluralis* ohne einen Nominativ gebraucht, als aiunt, dicunt, man sagt, wobey homines fehlt. Auch kann *philosophi, rhetores, oratores cet.* fehlen, wenn von einer solchen Materie die Rede ist: als virtutem *praecipiunt* propter se ipsam esse amandam man sagt, man müsse die Tugend um ihrer selbst wegen lieben: eigentlich sie sagen scil. philosophi. Wir sagen im Deutschen auch:

Schwabacher was unsightly, and he ousted the script from the palettes of the printing houses. He replaced it, as a means of differentiation in Fraktur, with the spacing-out of words, a legacy we struggle to eliminate today. Here is the reason why we find letterspaced words rather than italic used for emphasis in roman texts, but only in Germany, Switzerland and Austria. Roman must not be letterspaced anywhere, except for uppercase letters and small capitals.

Scheller in 1782 used roman and italic for Latin words. The enviable author and typesetter had at his disposal four different fonts of the same size for four categories of words. It appears that small caps were even rarer in Germany then than they are today. Otherwise, Scheller could have used them as well, had that become necessary. But there was no need – and in any case, no author should use more than four different fonts in any one text. In a grammar, more may be fine, but hardly in another book, never mind how scientific it is. A typographer of today faced with the task of setting a grammar in roman would have only three kinds of type at his disposal, namely roman, italic and small caps. Need of an additional variety would force him to use semibold letters. (Had

he used a sanserif as the basic font, he'd be lost even sooner.)
And how much better-looking a combination is Alte Schwabacher and Breitkopf Fraktur than Garamond and semibold
Garamond! Scheller in his grammar book perfectly presents
the difference between German and Latin through the clever
use of contrasting shapes, Fraktur and Schwabacher on the
one hand, roman and italic on the other. Had the grammar
book been set in roman, the Latin words would not stand out
as they do. Setting a grammar book is a difficult task indeed.
As long as we continue to deny ourselves the use of Fraktur,
we simply cannot do as good a job as a typesetter of the eighteenth century.

This once again demonstrates that we lost a treasure
when we lost Fraktur. People printing in other languages
would have envied us, had they but known. It is a pity that
Fraktur, then and now, is being fought tooth and nail on the
one side and praised on the other, with both sides using arguments that are irrelevant; nobody speaks of the very special
aptness of Fraktur and Schwabacher for the long words so
frequent in German orthography, of the space-saving compactness, of the unique shape, which has its roots in specifically German and transalpine* line art. One only has to read
Jeremias Gotthelf, Gottfried Keller, the love poems of Mörike
and Goethe, or *Des Knaben Wunderhorn,* set in roman, to
sense that all of them may be unsuitably *dressed* up. But this

---

* Unfortunately I cannot find a more appropriate adjective than this.
Certain individuals in the recent past have given the phrase ‹Central European› a bad reputation; nor does it fit properly. Literally translated,
‹transalpine› means ‹beyond the alps›. The Romans coined the word,
hence its meaning for them, ‹north of the alps›. Conversely ‹cisalpine›,
literally ‹this side of the alps›, means, from the Italian perspective, ‹south
of the alps›. — JT

only as an aside. In the middle of the nineteenth century, faced with the task of setting in roman a technical book similar to that of Scheller's, one was compelled to reach for the semibold in addition to italic and small caps.

Italic is derived from the humanist epistolary script. It is a relative of roman, frequently runs a little narrower, is tilted to the right, is conspicuous mainly because of this directional contrast and, within the overall color of a page, it irritates no more than is necessary for its function. Small capitals are letters in the shape of uppercase but nearly in the size of lower case n. The authentic cuts of Garamond, as shown in the Frankfurt type specimen of Conrad Berner (1592), already include small capitals in five sizes.

Key words to be emphasized are likely to be set in italic. Small caps remain the domain of names of persons and at times of places also. Since the middle of the nineteenth century, in countries using roman, there have evolved a number of useful and generally binding rules which we have to adopt and learn if we want to use roman correctly. It would be absurd to develop our own rules. The existing ones have proved their usefulness over time and we may adopt them without question. Further, respect for readers of another language forbids us to do things differently from the rest of the world. Therefore we are not at liberty to use italic and small capitals any way we like. It is time to leave the baby shoes behind and learn to use italic and small caps correctly. Until now this has rarely been done.

Where Italic, Where Small Capitals?

Neither italic nor small capitals must be used, even in textbooks, if all they do is act as signals, as a means of synoptical organization. (If such signals are absolutely necessary, a fat asterisk before the key words will do the job.) Indeed, small caps and italics should not serve to emphasize a word but rather to clarify it and differentiate it from the rest. ‹Rubrication› of the text is done with the different kinds of headings and occasionally, with marginalia. The paragraphs indicate a break in the flow of thought. Only in the rarest of cases is it permissible to set a word or a sentence in italic if it is to be spoken somewhat louder than the rest. As the German word *Schriftsteller* (an author, literally a *word placer*) reveals, it is a part of the art of writing to emphasize a key word through correct placement within a sentence. Bold setting of partial or complete sentences, which flourishes in some newspapers, and indeed the obsession with highlighting almost half the words in a text, does not help the reader at all. He wants to comprehend, and instead he is made to feel feebleminded. By contrast, to typeset anything and everything in one size only and not to use italic at all betrays a reprehensible lack of courtesy for the reader and is indeed far worse than the use of too many font variations.

The first purpose of cursive is to delineate the names of books, magazines, works of art, houses and ships as they appear in the text. For this reason, these words don't receive quotation marks. It is also advisable to define words and sentences in foreign languages through the use of italic rather than quotation marks. This is a firm rule in English, French and many other orthographies.

Small capitals *always* require gentle spacing; otherwise they lose all legibility.

In bibliographies, the authors should always be set in small caps and uppercase letters, and the book titles in italic. Authors of magazine articles should be set in uppercase and small caps as well, the essay titles in roman, and the titles of the magazines again in italic. (Magazines are books.)

Proper names that are not generally known, as well as uncommon words or those used with reservation or figuratively, like *Hurenkinder* (literally ‹whore's children›, widows in the typographical sense), may be set in quotation marks using roman, not italic. An unusual expression that may require explanation is likely to end up in quotation marks as well.

Quotations are set in roman type and given quotation marks.

These rules correspond to the English and French method, and they are internationally valid. Their use is to be preferred over the arbitrariness so frequent in German-language books.

I'd rather not talk about semibold letters; I must warn you urgently against using them at all, except in glossaries and the like. They function as eyecatchers only and don't serve to differentiate.

If, perhaps in a foreword, italic is the basic type, then roman type is used for emphasis, not letterspaced italic.

There are people who reject any kind of differentiation in a text. They claim it causes a disturbance. However, these people pour out the baby with the bath water. One doesn't look at a block of text merely to look at it; one wants to be able to read it. A small irritation here and there not only facilitates comprehension of the written word, it also agreeably livens up a page. Perpetual annoyance by quotation marks instead of italic is not at all pleasant. Quotation marks have their place – in fact several places! But the fitting use of italic, small caps and quotation marks in a book requires strict self-discipline from author and editor alike, and some authors do not like to practise self-discipline.

Genuine and Fake Small Capitals

Only fonts used for printing books come with a complement of true small capitals, but not all of them do. A genuine small capital is a touch taller than the lowercase n, has been designed and cut especially for the bread-and-butter font and has a shape different from that of an uppercase letter. It is a little wider and more robust than a corresponding majuscule.

A typesetting house without true small caps has to make do with small-size uppercase letters. This rarely looks satisfactory. The ersatz letters are either a little too big or a touch too small, and they always look a little anemic compared to the common letters of the basic font. Moreover, mixing two sizes of the same font in a line is inconvenient, especially when it happens often.

Genuine small capitals in sizes 6, 8, 9 and 10 give a typesetter additional advantages that may be important. Six-point small capitals are at the same time minute ‹uppercase letters› that may be used for superior print jobs. Further, instead of only four uppercase sizes one now has on hand eight in the same font, a selection that offers subtle gradation. To own genuine small capitals is a must for the well-equipped shop.

6 SMALL CAPITALS	6 CAPITALS
8 SMALL CAPITALS	8 CAPITALS
9 SMALL CAPITALS	9 CAPITALS
10 SMALL CAPITALS	10 CAPITALS

Quotation Marks

First and foremost it is the spoken word that is enclosed in quotation marks. It is not strictly necessary to do this, nor is it beautiful, but it is more distinct than typesetting without these marks. Quotation marks are obviously not required in those bloated novels where address and reply always form a new paragraph. The break, especially when marked by an indent, shows clearly that someone else is speaking. Quotation marks are distinct, but they do not exactly contribute to typographical beauty – this is my judgment.

There is more than one kind of quotation mark. In Fraktur we meet with German goose feet – two commas at the beginning, two inverted commas at the end: „n“. Not even a small space between word and symbol! The same goes for roman, where (of course) roman commas are used. Like goose feet, they come in pairs. I should like to emphasize that in German the goose feet at the end must be inverted commas (") and not raised ones ("), which would make a double apostrophe.

Then there are the French goose feet or duck feet, *guillemets* («n»). They must not be used with Fraktur. Strictly speaking, they alone deserve the name goose feet because, it seems to me, the German variety bear no similarity to the footprints of a goose. In Germany the guillemets point inward »n«; in Switzerland they have to point outward «n». Except before letters with some meat on them – A, J, T, V, W – and after periods, they must always be set with a touch of spacing.

It is a matter of choice whether to use French or German goose feet with German text set in roman letters.

The matter becomes more intricate when one realizes that it isn't the same thing to enclose speech in quotation marks, or to introduce an unusual term or word. Some people change styles here. They use both kinds, «n» and „n“. Others will use one-half of the pair to introduce the uncommon, thus ‹n› or ‚n' (not ‚n'! In German, an apostrophe cannot become a quotation mark!) But, alas, what to do when there are no single guillemets ‹n› that correspond exactly to the paired ones «n»? These very desirable marks are missing from most fonts. Single goose feet are by far the best marks for enclosing speech. The baroque doublets can then be saved for other less frequent occasions.

A quote within a quote: some people set «–‚'–», others use «–‚‚"–», employing the variety not used otherwise. However, it is difficult to see why a change should be necessary at all. «–« »–» works very well, since in most cases the inner quote is a short one. My own choice is: ‹–« »–›, in keeping with my preference for simpler quotation marks ‹ ›.

The English differentiate between *single quotation marks* 'n' and *double quotation marks* "n". Many good English typesetters today prefer single quotation marks for the spoken word because the double quotation marks introduce an element of unrest into the type area. Here again a little spacing is recommended, lest the quotation mark become an apostrophe.

Most countries have their own variety of quotation marks and rules for their use. Information may be found in the style manuals.

On Leading

LEADING is the spacing between lines of type. Especially
in larger works like books and magazines, the calculation of
this blank space is of great importance for the legibility,
beauty and economy of the composition.

It is hardly possible to establish a set of general rules for
leading in job printing, advertisements and similar jobs of
small volume that fulfill the needs of the day. Perhaps only
this much: the more exit lines or lines of differing lengths,
that is, the more turbulent the text block, the more leading
should be used. It emphasizes the linearity of the lines and
thus compensates for the disturbances in the outline or sil-
houette.

Poor typesetting – that in which the setting is too wide –
may be saved if the leading is increased. The loosely set books
of the late nineteenth century would look much worse if one
decreased the leading, which was generally quite substantial
at the time. Strong leading causes overly large gaps between
words to appear somewhat smaller.

Even the most substantial leading, however, does not
abrogate the rules of good word spacing. Large gaps between
words are no longer quite so obtrusive and irritating when
the leading is ample, but this is no excuse to use en-quad spacing or more between words.

The first obligation of a good typesetter is to achieve a
compact line image, something best accomplished by using

three-to-em or three-space word spacing. In former times even roman was set much tighter than we do it today; the specimen sheet that contains the original of Garamond's roman of 1592, printed in 14-point, shows a word spacing in all lines of 2 points only, which is one-seventh of an em! This means that we cannot call three-to-em word spacing particularly tight.

On the other hand, if the leading is as large, or larger even, than the font size, it is quite permissible to set a little wider than would be customary in tight typesetting, lest the words come too close optically and thus diminish the readability of the whole.

One is not always conscious of the fact that different typefaces require different leading. Single lines set in the more robust Fraktur, Schwabacher and some display types must be set tightly (larger sizes spaced even closer than three-to-em) lest the lines fall apart. Nor do these dark scripts tolerate much leading. They have to create an impression of compactness. This observation is also valid for older roman faces such as true Garamond, although here a little more leading usually does no harm. The situation is quite different when we consider the younger or neoclassical roman and Fraktur scripts of the eighteenth and nineteenth centuries, like the Bodoni, Didot and Walbaum romans, and Unger Fraktur. Compressed, they do not look good at all. They demand plenty of leading. It is not possible to convert a fine page set in Garamond into a Bodoni page without doing damage; the latter will likely require more leading. It follows that books with tight or compressed typesetting demand an older roman and books with ample leading need a younger one.

Leading in a piece of work similar to a book depends also on the widths of the margins. Ample leading posits wide borders in order to make the type area stand out. When set in an older roman, one and the same text block in a book may have narrower or wider margins; in the first case the book will appear more unpretentious, in the second it will look magnificent.

Books that contain sequential text as well as illustrations are a species apart. Here the overriding concern must be for perfect harmony between text area and illustration. Ideally, the type area should be worked out beforehand and sent to the illustrator so that he can then match picture and page image. If the drawings exist already, then the typesetter must try to create a text block that goes well with the illustrations. It is particularly difficult to find a suitable text block outline which agrees with bold woodcuts, as distinct from wood engravings. Old Schwabacher is often the script of choice in such a case. The work is considerably more difficult if roman is required. A larger size of type may sometimes help to overcome the dilemma. An older cut of semibold roman is out of the question for a beautiful book; a younger, meaty roman will appear quite dark but won't agree with woodcuts in general.

It is nearly impossible to say anything universally valid about the correct line spacing of modern ‹designer› faces. Less leading may be possible if the face approaches an older roman in style. Conversely, those similar to a younger roman may require more space. A final decision can be made only on the basis of sample page proofs.

Lastly, it is the length of the line, the number of letters in it, which exerts an influence on the leading. Lines over 24 ciceros (26 picas) in the bread-and-butter sizes almost always demand leading. Longer lines naturally need more, because the eye would otherwise find it difficult to pick up the next line. Such long lines are not good anyway; wherever possible one would make an effort to set narrower or to use two columns, or one would employ a larger size of type.

In the final analysis, a fixed and ideal length for the lines in a book does not exist. Nine centimetres (20 ciceros or 21 picas) is a good width provided the petit to garamond (8 to 10 point) sizes are being used. This width is not sufficient for the pica (12 point) size of a roman, however. And although it has erroneously been praised by some as an ideal length for a line in a book, nine centimetres looks abominable when the type size is large, because good line justification becomes almost impossible.

Typesetting Superscript Numbers
and Footnotes

To BEGIN with, let us enumerate what is repulsive and therefore wrong:

1. In superscript numbers in the text of books:
   a. An unsuitable font of superscript numbers;
   b. Superfluous parentheses following the superscript number;
   c. No spacing between word and superscript number.
2. In the footnotes:
   a. Reference numbers that are much too small, frequently illegible, and often belong to a different and discordant font;
   b. Deletion of the punctuation mark following the note number;
   c. The 4-pica flush-left rule often placed above the footnote, which is both unnecessary and unsightly;
   d. Insufficient leading within or between footnotes;
   e. Lack of clarity due to lack of indents.

Following this enumeration, here are reasons, remedies and an example:

1a. The cut used for superscript numbers must be the same as the basic font or, at the very least, closely related to it. Where old-style roman has fallen into disuse, superscripts of this style are almost never suitable. They do not fit a Walbaum or a Bodoni.

In linotype setting, 6-point lining numerals of the basic font may be used. It is not important whether lining or ranging numerals are used; both are suitable as long as they stem from the basic font or are similar to it. Lining numbers are preferred.

1b. A parenthesis after the numeral may be present in the manuscript copy, but it is superfluous everywhere else. It disturbs the type area for no reason and bothers the reader.

1c. Good typesetting demands a hairspace between superscript and word; otherwise the number doesn't stand out. It must not cling to the word.

2a. Fraction-size superscript numbers must not introduce the footnotes themselves. Sizes like 8-point, or worse, 6-point, numerators are so small as to be illegible, and footnote numbers have to be distinct because one is looking for them. Here, superscript numbers don't make sense and are a disease, while in the text, they should be small, and fraction-size numbers are appropriate. Since one should be able to find a footnote quickly, the normal number in the type size of the footnote must be used, never a superscript number.

2b. This note number is of normal shape and size, and it is followed by a full stop as an indispensible punctuation mark. To separate the number any further from the note is neither necessary nor beautiful; it is correct to indent the first line with a quad of the type size.* In my opinion,

---

* This is the practice Tschichold followed in the German edition of this book, where the notes are few. But his sample (p. 126), suggesting a book with many notes, is differently designed. There the notes begin flush left and runover lines are indented. – R B

to use the size of the text indent in the footnotes as well isartificial and obsolete; however, there may be exceptions when this older rule can be useful.

2c. There is no explanation for the survival of the 4-pica flush-left rule above a footnote. It is more superfluous than an appendix for a human being. Perhaps it exists to separate the footnote from the text, to introduce the note. But the smaller type size effects that distinction already. If separation by a line is absolutely required, then the line should run the full width of the text block.

2d. A page is completely harmonious only when text and footnotes have the same amount of leading. If the text is set in 10-point, with 2-point leading, the notes are set in 8-point, also with 2-point leading. While it is not entirely wrong to use one point less leading for the footnotes than for the text, a difference more pronounced than this causes the notes to be noticeably darker than the text and therefore is not good.*

One must not scatter additional leading between the paragraphs of a book text; nor should this be done between the footnotes on a page.

2e. Whoever indulges in the frivolous belief that he can make do without indents will suffer the consequences when the footnotes are to be set. The amateurish separation of footnotes and text with a few points of leading, occasionally even a single point only, results in a text block which is disarticulated, highly complicated, unrhythmical and therefore ugly. The procedure is as reprehensible

---

* *Tschichold's rule presupposes metal type, in which the smaller sizes are customarily not photographic reductions of the same master pattern used for the text sizes.* – R B

Was etwa die Abschrift der Enzyklopädie *De naturis rerum* des R A B A N U S M A U R U S zeigt[176], ist ein buntes Panoptikum aller Wunder dieser Welt, ein Bilderbuch voll naiver Freude an grünen Pferden und blauhaarigen Menschen[177].

Aber auch außerhalb dieser Handschriftengruppe herrscht im elften Jahrhundert lange in den Figuren der unruhige Geist eckig-gebrochener Zeichnung, mit zackiger Faltenbildung und reiner Zeichenstil[178] mußte er sich auch in den Schriftformen auswirken. So ist also Kompromiß mit dem Streben nach Regel und Zucht in der Schriftgestaltung das entstanden, was man als beneventanische ‹Brechung› bezeichnet hat.

Es ist kaum eine grössere Veränderung der Federführung dazu nötig gewesen als die Vollendung der Sagittalwendung, die schon in früherer Zeit erkennbar ist. Keineswegs ist die Tatsache der ‹Brechung› nur aus einer solchen ‹eigenartigen Druckverteilung›[179] zu begründen, wie M E N T Z und T H O M P S O N[180] dies tun. Allerdings kann man dafür anführen, schon die ersichtlich kurze Federfassung[181] sei dazu angetan, im Sinne der Bereicherung beziehungsweise der Zerlegung der Formen zu wirken.

176. (A. M. A M E L L I) ‹Miniature della enciclopedia Medioevale di Rabano Mauro dell'anno 1023› (*Documenti per la storia delle miniature e dell'iconografia*, 1896). Vgl. daraus unten Tafel 7.
177. B E R T A U X a.a.O.200; ‹C'est l'image du Monde, dessinée et colorée par un enfant.›
178. G. L A D N E R in *Jahrbuch d. Samnl. des ah. Kaiserhauses N.S.5* (1931), 45,65.
179. M E N T Z a.a.O.124.
180. A.a.O.355.
181. Vgl. unten Tafel 7.

Sample for superscripts and footnotes

as the practice of typesetting even simple texts without indents to mark the beginnings of paragraphs. It results in exactly the opposite of shape: mis-shape.*

A few peculiarities may be noted now.

If a book contains only a single footnote, or perhaps an isolated note here and there, then it would look quite peculiar if the numeral one were used over and over again to link text and note. In cases like this an asterisk should be used. In all other cases numerals are the choice.

No spacing should separate asterisk and word in the text; in the footnote, however, an asterisk must be followed by a 2-point space.

Footnotes consisting of a single word or of a few words only may be moved to the center of the page; this augments the harmony of centered typesetting. If there is more than one footnote on the same page, then the centering of a short one is not correct.

It can happen that a page contains many short footnotes which, placed one beneath the other, would disturb the balance between opposite pages. In cases like this it is better to have them following one another, separated by an em quad. All footnotes must end with a period.

Excessively long footnotes may be divided between opposite pages, but this practice must not be carried too far.

Should the type area be quite wide and set in 12-point or even larger size, one should consider setting the footnotes in two columns. One column having one line more than the other is a lesser evil than any attempt to obscure the difference between the two with additional leading.

* *German* Gestalt, Ungestalt. – H H

Footnotes are the latest and most highly developed form of annotation. Marginal notes require a substantial margin, whether it is needed for the book or not. Often it is difficult to find the next marginal note, in particular when a long one stretches over several pages. Marginal notes are obsolete.

For a number of reasons, it is not recommended to begin the numbering of notes anew on each page with the numeral one. It is better to number the footnotes of a book from beginning to end, or at least those of individual chapters. Only this method prevents notes losing their correct place. Nor is it wrong to combine the notes at the end of a chapter or of the entire book, though there may be times when this makes reading enjoyment difficult.

A flawlessly produced book can be identified by the fact that the last line of the footnotes aligns precisely with the last line of a normal text page. Such books, alas, are rare birds indeed.

Ellipsis Points

Their Function

Ellipsis points indicate that either a few letters of a word or one or more words have been omitted.

Grammar calls this omission of words ellipsis. Not every writer achieves Laurence Sterne's mastery of ellipses. Like the em dash, ellipses frequently disguise a writer's impotence to express himself. In most cases they are expendable.

A poet writes:

> *I do not know what it could mean*
> *that I am saddened so.*
> *A fable out of ancient times,*
> *it comes from nothing I have known.**

An ellipsis clown:

> *I do not know what it could mean*
> *that I am saddened so....*
> *A fable out of ancient times,*
> *it comes from nothing I have known....*

No doubt there are places where the nuance provided by ellipsis points is appropriate and necessary. The voice hangs

---

* *Heine, « Lorelei »: Ich weiss nicht, was soll es bedeuten, / Dass ich so traurig bin / Ein Märchen aus uralten Zeiten, / Das kommt mir nicht aus dem Sinn.*

suspended and retains the same pitch, while before a period it descends. Yet it takes a master of the word to put to use these delicate shadings, and more often than not ellipsis points become a disturbing mannerism. (How vague this sentence, had I ended it with three dots! I set down what I wanted to say and can say; three dots would leave it up to the reader to remain in the field and pick more flowers. When I am convinced I have picked them all, courtesy forbids sending the reader on another chase.)

Throughout the eighteenth and well into the beginning of the nineteenth century, asterisks were used to indicate letters omitted in a name: Madame de R***. Today this is considered outmoded. A writer would use omission points here, or merely a full stop.

Typesetting

In cases where single letters have been omitted to disguise an opprobrious word or name, as many periods (points) are set as there are letters missing, to show the knowledgeable whether they have guessed correctly. If no such consideration is given and three ellipsis points are set consistently, then the cloak cannot be lifted in most cases.

Whether one or more words have been omitted, in every case only three ellipsis points are set, even when the manuscript indicates four or more. Here and there one sees only two points printed; this is indistinct and fraught with danger. Three ellipsis points only is correct.

The customary way of printing these points is not satisfactory. Firstly, they tear holes into the text block if they are spaced, which is usually the case. They should be set without any spacing. Secondly, there is no logic in having letterspacing between omission points that indicate words. A word must be followed by the full word spacing of the line. We conclude: *The three ellipsis points must be set without spacing, and before them sits the full word spacing of the line:* ‹But ... I don't want to describe it.› *If a punctuation mark follows the omission points, it is to be separated from the last point by a one-point space:* ‹But no ... , she did not refuse, and I led her to the door of the wagon shed.›

Omission points indicating individual missing letters should not be spaced either; and, naturally, no spacing must precede them.

Ellipsis points set without spacing contribute to – and maintain – a good text block image.

Dashes

Their Function

One rarely finds a dash* replacing an unexpressed thought. Usually it indicates a small break, perhaps a kind of pause for reflection. Perhaps the German name should be changed: *Denkpause,* thought pause, instead of *Gedankenstrich,* thought line. Occasionally we find a dash at the end of a sentence where it serves to hide an embarrassing word or situation. If the name *Gedankenstrich* really fit, and if, further, a dash always concealed a thought, then one could imagine a book containing nothing but dashes. It is truly astonishing that neither the em-dash swindlers nor the ellipsis-point tricksters have hit on the idea.

It is often much better to see a comma in place of a dash: He came – but reluctantly. He came, but reluctantly. A dash is less superfluous in certain interpolations: I'll tell you – pay attention! – where to go. At times a dash separates address and reply: Listen, someone's knocking. – Take a look who's there. Then again, a dash may be used in place of parentheses, so as not to weaken the enclosed words: Garamond – the most common typeface of our day – and Bodoni are antithetical if we look at the laws that govern their shapes.

The dash – like the semicolon and quotation marks – is a recent symbol, not found in old and ancient literature. Goethe

---

* *German* Gedankenstrich, ‹*thought line*›. – H H

132

and his time rarely had a need for it. Even today it is frequently expendable and should be replaced with commas or parentheses wherever possible.

Typesetting

The widely used em dash is a blunt line one em long. This is far too much length and invariably spoils any cultivated type area. The situation could be remedied somewhat by diminishing the word spacing of the line before and after an em dash, but this is easily overlooked.

The only right thing to do is to use lines of half the length, en dashes, and separate them from adjoining words by using the word spacing normal to the line. These en dashes are also called distance lines because they represent the word *to* in distance or route indications: Basel–Frankfurt; no word spacing is used here.

In Monotype fonts, en dashes are part of the normal complement. For Linotype, they can be specially ordered. A manufacturer of books who desires flawless typesetting may and must insist on en dashes.

An exception now and again merely calls attention to the fact that en dashes are almost always missing in handset type. Yet there is a great need for them, especially in highly original script. It is one of the riddles of our time why they are not included with every font and in exactly the right size. Some handsetters suffer from the delusion that a hyphen can replace a dash as long as word spacing is used before and after. This is an error. A hyphen is too short.

Shape of the Dash

A thin, blunt line is sufficient as a rule. More specifically, the line should be as strong as the horizontal line in the letter e of the type size used. Unfortunately, this is not the case in unserifed and slab-serifed fonts, where the dash often does not attain the thickness of the horizontal line in the letter e. In most Fraktur and Schwabacher scripts, the strength of the dash is correct. Some typesetters feel that they should use a significantly bolder line (lifted from sanserif, perhaps), because the one-em dash, much too long, leaves a rather disturbing hole in the type area. But a bolder line is not the answer; the shorter en dash is. Except with unserifed and slab-serifed fonts, it is a stylistic error to use a thicker line.

There is only one circumstance where the em dash may be used and is indeed necessary: in price tables.

The purpose of these words is to draw attention to a detail in typesetting rarely considered, and to contribute to the removal of an eyesore that is all too frequent.

Whore's Children
and Cobbler's Apprentices

DOUBTLESS all textbooks of typesetting warn that the exit line of a paragraph at the head of a book page must be avoided at all cost. And indeed such a line insults the eye and the mind. The exit line destroys the rectangle of page and text block, and the meagre end portion of a sentence looks paltry.

The rule is correct. But rarely does the textbook explain how to get rid of these widows, which in German are called *Hurenkinder,* whore's children. They present no problem to someone using two points of leading between paragraphs here, and three or four there. But this kind of typesetting does not produce good book typography.

The careful publisher above all wants to see tight typesetting. The question then is, can widows be avoided at all? Rarely is it possible to squeeze them out or to draw them in without despoiling a uniform set. Is it permissible to ask the author to don his creative cap and add a few words, or delete some, to surmount a typographical complication? I think not. The better the text, the more difficult it is. Moreover, it isn't the typesetter who is master of the text, it is the author. Should the poet no longer be alive, we could not ask him in any case.

Let us assume the poet to be dead or otherwise out of reach. Better yet, let us be convinced that it would be wrong to ask the writer to make changes solely for the sake of a more pleasing typographical image. This being the case, we then take another look at the adjoining pages. Is there really nothing we can tighten a little, or space out perhaps? Possibly we can save a line at the beginning of the chapter by moving the first paragraph up? The best method is to simply shorten the preceding page by a line. Of course, there will now appear a blank line at the foot, but it does not disturb provided the running head sits at the head of the page, the margins are not extremely small and we are dealing with a single column only.

Or we make an exception and lengthen a page by one line. But this works only in books with sufficiently wide margins. (See page 114–115 in this book.)

Nothing can be said against ‹widows› that show up beneath the continuous line under a running head. In cases like this the page rectangle remains undisturbed.

It is a foolish stunt to shorten a page by one line and then lead out the text to regain the old height. This destroys line registration, which is the trademark of good page make-up.

There is never a need to produce widows.

Typographic orphans, which in German are called *Schusterjungen*, cobbler's apprentices, are altogether different. Some people spurn the first line of a new paragraph at the bottom of a page. It would seem to me, however, that avoiding it can be no more than wishful thinking. One should not demand too much. Such a wish could easily have been realized at a period in typesetting when almost any amount of spacing seemed permissible. This was before a tight and uniform set became the norm. Entry lines at the foot of a page may be unwanted, but they are permissible. It is only when paragraphs are leaded, and when there is an empty space above the single last line, that they become obnoxious. Some people fret over the indent when the page number sits on the bottom of the page, but unless the page number is centered, I usually indent it with the same number of points used for the text paragraphs.

Planning the Typographical Layout
of Books with Illustrations

THERE ARE two kinds of books with illustrations: those where the pictures are scattered throughout the text, and the other kind, where text and images form two parts of the same book.

The desire to keep type area and maximal image size the same (see figure 1) is just and can certainly lead to a harmonious book form. It is not so certain whether these picture sizes will meet our demands for clarity and distinctness; both will suffer as image reduction increases. There is no doubt, though, that the method is the only correct one when image and text are printed on the same kind of paper. The maximum image is the width of the type area; the maximum image height is the height of the type area minus 7 to 11 mm (2¾–4¼ in.) in for a one- or two-line caption, which has to remain within the type area.

When the proportions of the book are being considered, it must not be forgotten that most pictures, and paintings in particular, come in beautiful rectangular proportions. Formats approaching a square are infrequent. The image reduction inside a book usually increases due to the caption, which more often than not is necessary, and for which one or two lines should be saved, depending on requirements. Taken together, picture and caption form a slim rectangle which approaches the proportions of the Golden Section. Such a slender image area then requires a book format narrower

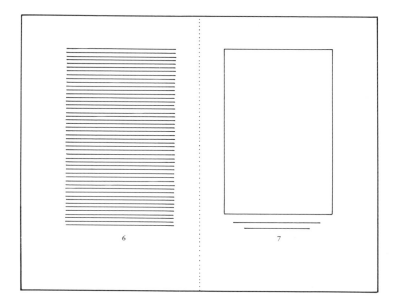

Figure 1.

than that offered by quarto proportion, which is a size frequently unsuitable for books with pictures. Only the format A4 has proved to be a good standard for books of this kind. An agreeable smaller format has a trim size of 16 × 24 cm; 6⁵⁄₁₆ × 9½ in.

After all this has been taken into account and a well-thought out pair of sample pages has been printed and approved, then one can go ahead and have an appropriate number of blank four-page text-block sheets made up, where the recto pages could look like those shown in our figure 4. These blank text blocks facilitate pasting during page make-up because image position and the appearance of a set of pages can be determined and settled once and for all.

Horizontal pictures also have to bow to the type area (fig-

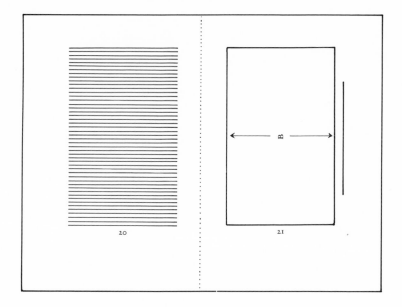

Figure 2.

ure 2). If the book has very broad margins, then the height (b)
of the picture can follow the width of the type area and the
caption can be placed in the margin. As a rule, though, the
caption should sit inside the type area and the picture should
be reduced in size accordingly (figure 3).

Generally, but especially with works of art, the original
image proportions should be retained. It would be a mistake
to alter them merely for the sake of completely filling a type
area. It cannot be demanded, therefore, that pictures always
fill the height and width of the space available. If all the pictures have the same proportions, then the height of the type
area is determined by the pictures, naturally without forget-
ting the captions beneath the plates.

Pictures of paintings and other works of art must never be

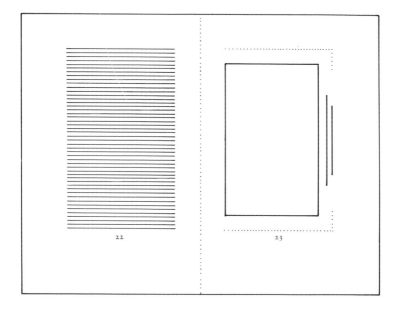

Figure 3.

trimmed. Because even the last millimetre in a picture has meaning, a platemaker may trim away only what is absolutely necessary. (Plates that require trimming must be a full 3 mm larger on the sides to be trimmed.) A work of art will be disfigured if it is presented in abbreviated form.

Books with illustrations scattered throughout are more expensive than those where the illustrations are kept together in a separate part. The most expensive method is to glue single illustrations onto pages, in particular if they show up in places other than the frontispiece or in the middle of a signature. The glue strip distorts the book page. It is less expensive and produces a better effect if quarter sheets are folded and inserted. Moreover, the irksome operation of pasting is eliminated.

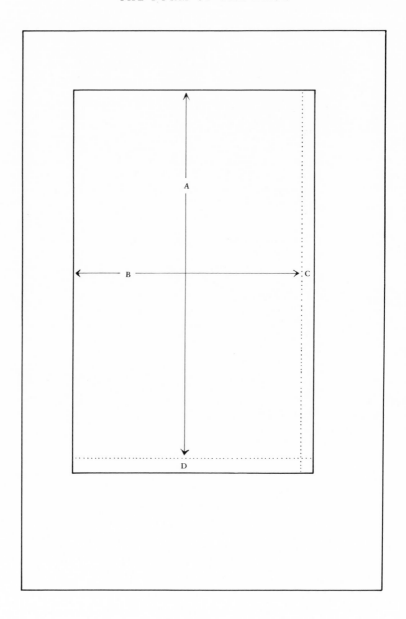

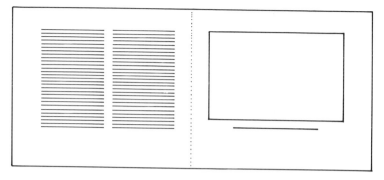

Figure 5.

As we can see in figures 1, 2 and 3, the position of the picture area has to be the same as that of the text block. The shared page margins should unite text page and picture page into one whole, because even a book with illustrations is still a book and thus subject to the basic law that the effect of a pair of pages is important. It is the spread, rather than the single page. If one feels, however, that the pictures are entirely separate from the book and should be placed in the middle of the page, then it doesn't make sense to have their size determined by the size of the text area. It must be kept in mind that the rule of designing a picture page like a text page also applies to horizontal illustrations (figure 2). It is a mistake to forget the rest of the book and place horizontal pictures in the middle of the page, independent of the text block.

Left, Figure 4. Sample diagram for books with illustrations. The bold line indicates the extent of the type area. A = *maximal height of a full-page illustration in portrait format,* B = *maximal height of a full-page illustration in landscape format. The difference* (C) *that makes up the full type area must equal the space of two lines, i.e. 7–11 mm. (2³⁄₄–4¹⁄₄ in.).*

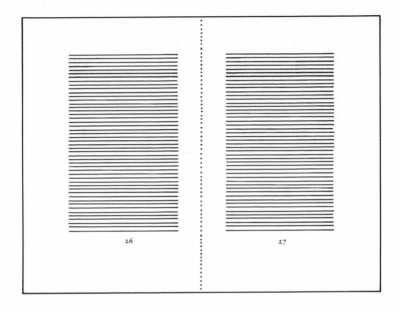

Figure 6a. Text area.

Horizontal pictures are always annoying and should be avoided. If it so happens that the majority of pictures for a book are horizontal, then it is better to choose a landscape format and set the text in two columns (figure 5).

To hold text and images to the same size is a rule that should be followed even when the pictures form a separate part of the book. It is likely, however, that the pictures will then appear too small. This is because the images are denser and thus darker than the type block, which is usually grey. A darker block of the same size always appears optically smaller. In this case it is entirely correct to use a somewhat larger type area for the picture portion, provided the geometrical proportions remain the same.

The position of the illustrations also depends on whether

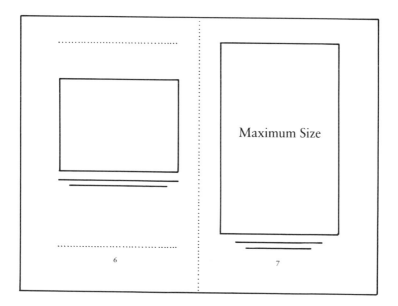

Figure 6b. Pages with illustrations in the same book. Larger type area, but in the same proportion as the text block.

they appear on the recto page only, or on both the recto and verso pages. Single-page printing produces an effect almost like tipped-in plates; if one has followed the classical rule of making the center margin half the width of the outside margin, the effect will now be exaggerated, and modification is called for. But in no case must the left and right margins be anywhere near equal in size. The empty white page to the left alone already demands from the image a certain proximity to the fold.

If both recto and verso pages have been printed, then one must not stray far from the rule that the inner margin of a page should be half as wide as the outer one. Otherwise the pair of pages will fall apart, which does not have to be the

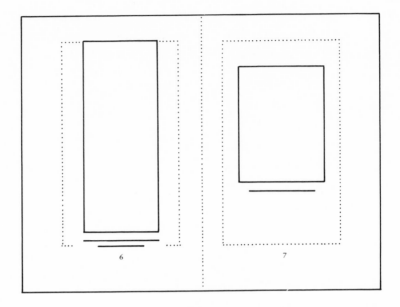

Figure 7.

case even if they are quite dissimilar (figure 6b). Computing
the illustrations is done on the basis of a printed scheme or
grid (figure 4), which gives the maximum measurements.
Page make-up is accomplished by pasting the prints on the
grid, which fixes the height of the illustration on the page.
Tall pictures fill the text area vertically and are centered horizontally (figure 7, left) in order to retain registration; smaller
pictures (figure 7, right) must be positioned in such a way
that the ratio between the blank spaces at top and bottom
corresponds to 1:2 or 3:5.

In all cases the captions remain with the pictures. While it
would be possible to leave them at a constant height – that is,
near the foot of the picture block – this is permissible only in
unusual cases. If the pictures should be numbered, as indi-

cated in figure 7, then the position of the number should be the same for all plates, and they have to register exactly. Occasionally one sees books where illustrations are numbered

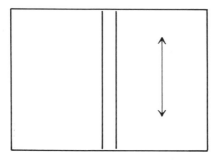

Figure 8.

at top right (outside the print area). To do it this way is expensive and seldom correct. It is not book-like and makes typesetting costly. Even when printer and typesetter take the greatest of care always to place the number in precisely the same spot, some later movement left, right, up or down during the folding process is inevitable.

If a difference is desired between plate number and folio, then cursive can be used or the text page number could be adorned with parentheses. If the plates are larger than the text block, as we assume them to be in figure 7, then the picture numbers will sit a little lower and to the outside anyway when compared with the folios.

The important thing is that even plates of different sizes have to be printed in accordance with the governing type area. They must not be positioned ‹by feel›. It follows that it is the job of the typesetter or compositor to adjust the plates and produce uniformly large pages, to determine and fix the effect before the matter goes to the printer. The first picture

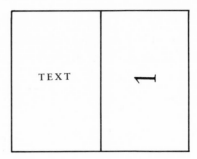

Figure 9a. Landscape format illustration opposite a text page.

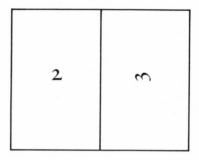

Figure 9b. A normal picture and one at right angles.

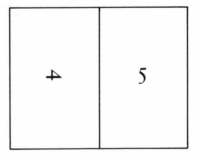

Figure 9c. A picture at right angles, left, and a normal one, right (not as good as B, and usable only in exceptional cases). The head of the picture ends up in the gutter! And case C cannot be combined with case D, following.

proof sheet should be returned trimmed to size, but not otherwise corrected, for a last check on the widths of the margins; the position of the pictures themselves should not require any more changes at this stage.

Works containing color plates are proliferating in the marketplace, and it simply has to be said: it is an absurdity to reproduce a painting the area of a window or larger in the size of a post card. Those are no longer reproductions, they are fakes, no matter whether they are done well or poorly. If these drastic reductions are really necessary, then it is invariably better to reproduce in black-and-white. Color should always be reproduced as large as possible, and it is better to present details rather than the whole. A color reproduction linearly reduced to one-half or one-quarter of the original may still be satisfactory. Beyond that, detail prints should be made, and preferably of original size.

To escape the dilemma posed by horizontal pictures, nearly square book shapes have recently been used, a move

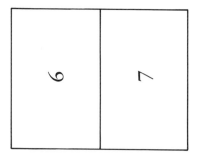

Figure 9d. Two pictures, both at right angles, must both be legible from the right side of the book. Reversing picture 6 would be an annoying solution, because the reader would have to turn the book twice.

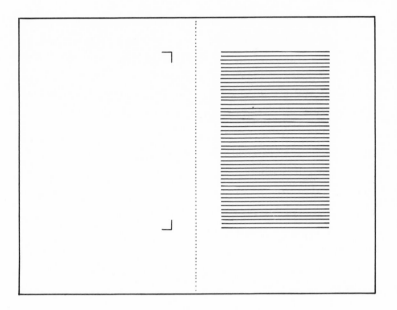

Figure 10a.

that has to be opposed. Truly monstrous books have been produced that give every bibliophile the creeps. (See also page 149.)

The *grain of the paper* is of the greatest importance, and the paper for illustrations, like the text paper, has to run in the direction of the spine of the book (figure 8). One must not believe that a single sheet running the wrong way doesn't really matter. Even isolated inserts and wraps will curl in to the well-known transverse folds as a consequence of incorrect grain direction. The reason why a book or magazine is difficult to open or close is always grain running the wrong way either in some of its parts or in the entire book (text paper, plates, endpapers, cover). It is never the fault of the bookbinder, as many people tend to think.

The Position of Horizontal Plates

If horizontal pictures are unavoidable, then at the very least one should be able to look at them comfortably. Consequently, there are certain guidelines. The large numbers in figures 9a to 9d indicate how the picture should be seen.

Plates Mounted on Art Card or Paper

Plates that are to be mounted may be cut only if they are ordinary photographs. The reproduction of a flat piece of art (a painting, graphic art) must never be closely trimmed. A narrow white border 2 mm wide should be left, lest the trimming abbreviate everything and cause a distorted picture. Borders narrower than 2 mm tend to be uneven.

The caption belongs on the background paper. It doesn't look good on the plate paper itself. It is entirely feasible to place the caption near the foot on the opposite page, provided picture and text area have the same height. The plate may gain by doing this. Corner marks for the bookbinder, who will tip in the plates, must be printed on the background paper also. They have to be placed *sideways* near the inner margin or gutter (top and bottom, figures 10a and 10b). Typesetting and printing of background sheets demands much attention from compositor and printer.

If the text paper has sufficient stability, it may be used for background paper, provided the reverse remains blank. Other background papers (art card) have to be extremely pliant so as not to stand up from the open book. For this reason alone the grain must run in the right direction. Wrong grain results in board-like stiffness and transversal folds during binding.

The best tint for the background paper is the shade used

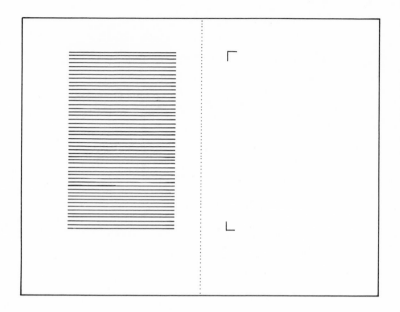

Figure 10b.

for the text paper. Color reproductions of paintings and similar art work, where it is important that the true color be recognizable, should be mounted only on a white or chamois
colored background. To use darker backgrounds and deeply
colored ones is a bad habit that arose at the beginning of our
century. It almost always interferes with the true impression
of a color picture. Brown and green backgrounds are the
most harmful, while black and clay-grey, *i.e.* neutral, un-
colored tones, are somewhat more bearable. But the best is a
white that matches that of the text paper. (Presentations of
typographical works may break this rule. A lightly tinted background paper is acceptable in this place since it stands in for
the random background on which we might otherwise see the
work. Yet even here a common white is often better than
shaded or tinted paper, but not a bright white.)

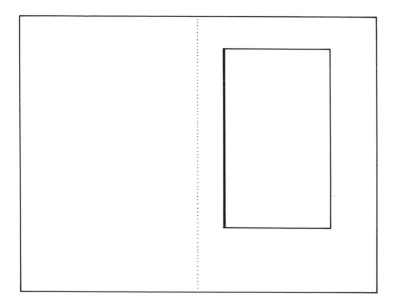

Figure 11.

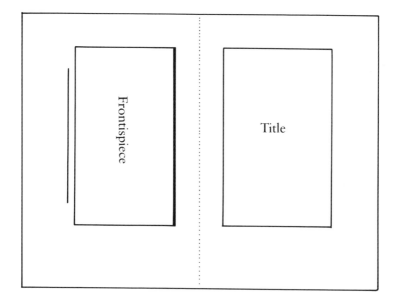

Figure 12.

To repeat, if color plates are to be mounted, the best background is chamois or a lightly tinted white. Dark backgrounds are a poor legacy of the time before 1914. Luckily, we hardly ever see an ornamental frame or colored border strips around a reproduction any more.

It goes without saying that the grain of both reproduction and background must run the right way (see Figure 11).

The Mounting of Reproductions

In nine out of ten mounted reproductions, the glue has been applied in the wrong place, namely at the upper edge. It also shows total incompetence if glue has been applied only at the two upper corners. The bond will go first at the outer corner, then the plate shifts and is ruined or even lost. At the very least the entire edge must be glued, but this, as we know, is wrong. Worse yet is to fasten the plate at three corners only; invariably, squeeze folds are the result. The single correct procedure is to apply glue to the vertical edge nearest the spine (figure 11). The bold line is the glue strip. Only this guarantees that the inner corners will not bend over (as they do when the picture has been wrongly mounted). The rule applies even if a horizontal picture has been chosen for the title page (figure 12). The reason why the ‹top› of the plate must border the inner margin or gutter has been given elsewhere already. The ‹bottom› must not face the title opposite.

And finally we should point out that the last plate in a book must not be a horizontal one and that the two last pages following the plate section should remain blank, just like the first two pages of the first print sheet. This is something that is usually thought of too late, if at all.

Headband, Trim-Edge Color,
Endpapers and Marker Ribbon

ONCE UPON a time, when books were still being bound by hand, one used to reinforce the spine of the book-to-be at both head and foot with a strip of parchment that was sewn on by hand with either cotton or silk thread. Originally this was done to fasten together the ends of the signatures, to provide resistance to the finger hooking a book from the shelf, and to furnish protection for the head of the leather cover or case. The foot was protected in the same way for symmetry's sake.

Glued instead of sewn headbands began to appear at the beginning of the nineteenth century, with the Industrial Age. The Barbou volumes of the eighteenth century still have genuine sewn headbands, while books of the early nineteenth century show the ersatz modifications necessary to facilitate mass production: a strip of cloth enfolding a string, glued together and forming the torus-like bulge that covers up the notches formed by the layers of folded sheets. Or in the same technique is used with colored paper in place of the cloth.

The commercial headband as we know it today appeared at some time during the second half of the nineteenth century. It is made from woven cloth and available in a rather poor selection of colors and patterns. Usually it is cut to the width of the spine and then folded and glued to it at both head and foot. The colored fold is supposed to cover the ends of the layers of paper. No longer is there a technical function or a necessity to do this. It is merely decoration.

This is ‹decoration› of a kind we see in a frayed, sloppily knotted and mismatched necktie. For it is very difficult, even looking at books that have never been used, to find one where the headband a) has exactly the right length, b) is not frayed at one end or the other, c) has been glued on straight, d) really sticks to the spine and e) harmonizes with the general color scheme. Sometimes it even peeks over the edge of the book, perhaps because the fold is thicker than allowed by binding edges that are too scanty.

As far as I am concerned, I prefer books without a headband. They look much neater than those where the fabric hardly ever fits and is frayed to boot. How about calling them fraybands?

It isn't that the headband is entirely without merit. There are places where it offers a welcome opportunity for decoration. But more often than not it is expendable. We have here an atavism as difficult to be rid of as the human appendix. As far as books are concerned, it's really simple enough: use a pair of pincers.

We can live with the fact that the headband is rarely fastened down securely. But if it's been cut exactly to size, rest assured it's frayed, which makes it unpleasant.

Why does the thing have to be made from rayon or artificial silk? Surely it is easy today to manufacture a non-fraying, easily cut headband from plastic. The part to be glued should be perforated and the visible portion rippled or otherwise beautified to get rid of the rubber tube look – it would solve the problem of sullied headbands once and for all!

As long as the materials exist, it is possible to use leather, colored paper, or linen strips for more expensive editions.

The material has to be glued around a piece of string which then causes the bulge in the fold. While paper, leather and linen require a lot of rubbing for the glue to stick, they are not likely to fray. But if no fraying occurs and the headband really adheres, then it is probably the color of the headband which doesn't match the rest of the book and gives rise to renewed desperation; presumably the order number was found by drawing lots in the stock room. Is it really a secret that the color of the headband cannot be left to chance or accident, and that interaction with its surroundings has to be taken into account? A purely white headband is a no-no when the book paper is tinted; either it has to have the same shade or it has to stand out because of its different color. The visible narrow strip of a headband may be welcome as a contrasting teaser – a brown binding should look good with a green headband – but of course, it's all a question of subtlety and nuance! Headbands are so mismatched these days, it looks as if those responsible have forgotten about them and left selection to the reckless!

The matter becomes vastly more complex when we take into consideration the head trim-edge color of the book, or colored endpapers, and a colored ribbon bookmarker.

*

The reasons behind coloring the trimmed edge at the head of a book are purely practical: the pigment makes a better seal against dust from above and, since dust cannot be avoided, it provides a separate color to make dust less noticeable. Moreover, pure-white trim-edges don't look good, especially on big books. All-around trim-edge color is more beautiful than merely coloring the head, but it is rare today. Trim-edge color should be unobtrusive and carefully chosen to blend with the binding. We find the all-around glaring red of certain foreign pocket book editions highly repulsive.

Gold leaf and edge pigment, and the polishing of the gilt or colored edges, which is still done for special single volumes, all contribute greatly to sealing the trim-edge of a book.

Volumes that consist entirely of art paper, or where this has been inserted, permit neither coloring nor gilt edging because the pages would tend to stick to each other.

A colored head or all-around trim-edge is part and parcel of book exterior design. It can be done discreetly, in which case an off-yellow beige is almost always suitable, or a bolder color may be chosen, but then endpaper and headband must be taken into consideration.

*

First something about endpapers – in German the *Vorsatz,* ‹pre-set›, abbreviated from *Vorsatzpapier.* The *Vorsatz* is so called because it is set before the book proper and after). Yet the *Vorsatz* at the end of a book is not a *Nachsatz,* an ‹after set›; it is still called a *Vorsatz.* The English, entirely different from the Continentals as they always are, call it *endpaper.* They never say *frontpaper.*

It has almost been forgotten that endpapers may be colored. Wherever one looks there are white endpapers, perhaps because, regrettably, most books are printed on stark white stock, which is harmful to the eyes. Some people (obviously they are not quite with it) find the leap from a darker binding into the gleaming white of the contents too daring and choose an off-yellow endpaper. This does not always fit, because the color of the cloth binding it has to agree with is usually forgotten.

For all that, a colored endpaper could provide a pleasant

transition between cloth color outside and the hue of the paper inside. It could hide the annoying color shade variations of the inside of the cover or casing much better than the ersatz handmade paper now used for the purpose. Text stock is rarely appropriate for endpapers because it does not have sufficient surface sizing. The cloth used for binding has more pull than the paper. Ideally, they should be equal in strength; that is, the same stock could be used to cover the case and serve as endpaper as well, but this is rarely done. Quarto and larger formats look much better when the endpapers are colored rather than white. On the whole, a chamois-colored endpaper rarely ever goes well with white text paper.

*

The choice among bookmarker ribbons is even poorer than that for headbands, and their number hardly exceeds half-a-dozen. There are no narrow ribbons and only four or five different colors are offered — ugly ones at that — which never match anything, though this is hardly the reason why marker ribbons are seldom provided. If the print run warranted it, they could be manufactured in any width and color. They are simply not thought of as desirable items. In order to miss a marker ribbon one has to read a book now and again. To be read is the ultimate purpose of a book. For this reason better books should come equipped with marker ribbons.

It seems to me that trade books generally will have headbands. Thus we have a book cover, a headband, endpapers and a marker ribbon. Taken together, these fragments should enter into a color composition where each component noticeably relates to the other. But, alas, how rarely is this the case! The Cinderella is possibly the ribbon with its meagre assortment of six varieties: not a sufficient basis from which to begin the selection of the cover cloth! And because a white marker ribbon is not suitable for tinted text paper, it is left out, especially if the print run is too small to permit special fabrication. Larger runs allow this, however (silk is the material of choice, not rayon), and they can be made in any width and color!

As far as the available color shades of headbands are concerned, we can live with them. Cloth binding, endpapers and headband can now be combined into a pleasant and convincing color composition. To give detailed instructions here is not possible. Any attempt would turn into a theory of colors. It should be noted, however, that the number of possible good solutions is equal to the number of repulsive solutions already found.

Jacket and Wrapper

IT IS NOT likely that the oldest trade books, published at the end of the fifteenth and the beginning of the sixteenth century by Anton Koberger and Aldus Manutius, were given jackets. It seems that these first came into existence around the middle of the nineteenth century, when the production of books was industrialized. Their purpose was to protect the valuable binding, at least for a time. Different from the cover, the jacket bore the title of the book and often further particulars also on the front panel. At times this was merely a straightforward copy of the title page with, perhaps, a border drawn around it. In the first decades of our century it was the cover itself that, to its detriment, became the carrier of a marketing tool: the title.

In time, a separation evolved again between the book cover as the permanent integument, and the protective jacket as the carrier of advertising. It is regrettable that over the past thirty years the quality of book covers has declined; at the same time the design and form of the jacket, which lures the buyer, has been further and further refined.

A book jacket is a kind of poster. It is designed not only to draw attention but also to protect the cover from light, dirt and abrasions until the book is safely in the hands of the buyer. Publishers make book jackets not so much to present the buyer with a protective cover for his book but to guard themselves and the bookseller against loss. Carefully made books should never be distributed without a jacket, be it ever so humble.

A jacket is not an actual part of the book. The essential portion is the inner book, the block of pages. Even cover and endpapers, strictly speaking, are false parts, temporary only, because they will be discarded when the book is re-bound. The only valid book title sits inside the book, on the title page. Whatever is written on the jacket does not matter to the bibliographer; therefore it is not necessary and indeed an error to so much as mention the existence of a jacket. Like an advertising leaflet that has been inserted between the pages, a jacket is merely a floating addendum.

For the same reason, pictures on the jacket or protective cover and those glued to the cardboard slip case should neither be assumed to be nor described as genuine components of the book. If they constitute an essential part, they should be added to the inner book, perhaps in the form of a frontispiece. Pictures on the wrapper or the cover are soon damaged.

Those who do not trust their fingers to be clean may read a book while it is still protected by the jacket. But unless he is a collector of book jackets as samples of graphic art, the genuine reader discards it before he begins. Even the collector will remove the jacket and save it in a box. Books that are still inside their jackets cannot be held very well, and the visible advertising is annoying. The true garment of the book is its cover; the jacket is merely the raincoat. To protect the jacket itself with an additional one made from cellophane is about as ludicrous as wrapping paper around the protective cloth cover of an expensive leather suitcase.

In addition to author's name and title, the front of the jacket often holds the name of the publishing house and some advertising copy. Not infrequently we find these literary components embedded in a mawkish drawing or painting which at times bleeds around the spine to the back of the jacket. Presumably the artist is under the impression that the bookseller presents the jacketed volume out-spread in the display window; however, few booksellers avail themselves of this opportunity.

The flaps of the jacket should be as wide as possible. Frequently the front flap contains a blurb that outlines the contents of the book, or the publisher uses it and the back flap as well to advertise other books. Jackets of English books as a rule show the price at the foot of the front flap, which may be cut off if the book is to be given away – though it would be better to discard the jacket entirely. The jacket, mere servant of the cover, does not become any more ‹aristocratic› if flaps and back side are left blank. Since a buyer appreciates information about other books from the same publisher, one need not have scruples against covering the flaps, the back side, and possibly the entire and almost always blank inside or flip side of the jacket, with book ads and publisher's information. It is another question whether the print run of the book warrants the expense. Often it is more reasonable to print a complete list of available titles on thin paper and enclose it with the book. In no case need one make an effort to produce a jacket which, beyond the desired effect of an attractive front panel, is discrete and reserved. Beautiful, careful typesetting is not forbidden, but the jacket design should be such that it will be discarded without any misgivings once it has been read, like any brochure. This is the only way to counter the unpleasant habit of some people who, like a bookseller, put jacketed books on their shelves. (I will shelve a book that is still in its jacket only if the cover is even uglier than the jacket is. Unfortunately, there are more such every year!)

The lettering on the spine of the jacket should restate all essential information of the front panel. Experienced book buyers – those not compelled to pull every volume from the shelf – should be able to glean everything worth knowing from looking at the spine. It should tell them the author and title, and space permitting, it should give a few particulars about the editor or publisher, the number of pages, tables, plates and so forth, and also the name of the publishing house. The design of the jacket spine should be as attractive as that of the front panel itself.

Since the jacket is not part and parcel of the book, its design and graphic form need not necessarily follow the shape of the book. It is entirely permissible to enclose a noble and cultivated cover in a crass jacket designed solely for the purpose of attracting customers. On the other hand, any person of taste will be more kindly disposed toward the book if there is some coordination between jacket color and form, the case, and the book itself. The more expensive the book, the more durable and wear-resistant the jacket paper should be. Inexpensive books destined for a quick sale may have a jacket made from groundwood paper; precious books usually spend more time in a display window and should have jackets made from strong acid-free paper.

The printer needs an exact dummy of the finished book if he is to print a jacket that fits precisely; otherwise positional errors are unavoidable. The height of the finished jacket must match that of the cover to a hair. The jacket print run should be ten percent higher than that of the book so that damaged jackets may be replaced.

If the book comes in a simple slipcase, a cardboard box

(which, like the jacket, must be removed before the book ends up on a library shelf), then an advertisement may be glued to the display side and the book itself does not need a printed jacket. This is the preferred mode if the book has been very softly bound and cannot stand on its cover. Booksellers then display the box with the book inside.

Wrappers in the form of paper strips (‹cigar bands›) may be conspicuous, but they harm a book without a jacket. Sunlight will bleach the color from the exposed part of the book; soon the book will be unsightly and can no longer be sold. Only books with jackets may have ‹cigar bands› – which can also be simulated by overprinting.

On Books that are Too Wide,
Too Large, or Square

It isn't only the general handiness of a book that determines its absolute width; the depth of the average bookshelf must also be considered. Books wider than, say, 24 cm (9½ in.) are therefore irksome. Most people do not like to handle books that are so wide. They don't fit into the shelf, they lie around for a while until the owner gleefully palms them off, or else they end up in the wastepaper basket. One thinks, for instance, of the published histories of business firms who want to impress with size; almost invariably the title is missing from the spine, though here it may not matter much.

Those who want their books to last and who want them to be found again will neither make them excessively wide nor forget to put the title on the spine.

Legitimately wide books, those with large and valuable plates for instance, are a different story. The owner of these usually has a special place for them. But on the whole, one should not make books unduly large. One rarely encounters the reverse case: books that are too small.

Of late, books that are square have become fashionable in certain circles, among people who fancy themselves to be ultramodern. They like to do things differently. They use *sanserif* instead *of roman,* they favor flush-left beginnings and shun indispensable indents because they are alleged to bring unrest into a page; these are the people who like to use a square format.

Strictly speaking, a square format is less repulsive than, say, an excessively wide quarto format, which is simply plump like a hippopotamus. Here, an optically corrected square or even a pure square could be better.

But there are three arguments that speak against books whose format approaches the equal-sided rectangle. The first is simply handiness. It is difficult for an unsupported hand to master a square book – even more difficult than to hold the ugly A5 format. The second argument concerns storage. If these books are wider than 24 cm (9½ in.) they must be put down flat. Yet books should be capable of being stood upright on a shelf so that they can be found quickly and used.

For the final argument, I have to make a little detour. It is the hinges on either side of the spine that hold the inner book, the book block, in position. If the inner book is heavy – regrettably often the case – then the face of the book will drop, touch the shelf and begin to collect dust, a thing the edges of the cover are supposed to prevent. The longer the spine of the book relative to its width, the better the inner book will remain in position. The spine of an album in landscape (*i.e.* horizontal) format is no longer sufficient to fulfill this function. The situation is similar for books that approach a square format: the face of the inner book will soon touch the book shelf. It is for these reasons that square-format books should be rejected as modernizations that are fundamentally wrong.

Within the range of more plausible book sizes we have numerous proportions – that is, ratios between breadth and height. As long as sound tradition has been abandoned and must be established anew, we should begin at the beginning and examine the format of a book before we start working on it. We should investigate the geometrical proportions, to check whether the ratios are precisely 2:3, 3:4 or follow the Golden

Section, to mention a few of the more important ones.

More often than one might think, a simple proportion like 2:3 is the best; this goes even for quarto books, though one might have to have the paper specially made. There is no recipe, but much may be learned from books produced before 1790, even about proportions.

A last word that only borders on our theme: the weight of a book. Most of our books are much too heavy. Often the reason is art paper. Thick tomes of art paper should therefore be divided into two volumes. The old books were much lighter. Indeed, Chinese books can be called feather-light. The paper mills should make an effort to produce papers that are much lighter. This applies to art papers and offset papers in particular.

Printing Paper: White or Tinted?

RAW MATERIAL used for making paper has to be bleached chemically before it attains a stark white color. But unbleached paper is not only more durable, it is also more beautiful. Today it is very rare and shows up only in the form of handmade paper. The wonderful tone of our oldest printed books and – older yet – paper manuscripts has stood the test of time and remains as beautiful as ever, provided the books have not suffered from water damage or decay. When one praised ‹pure white› paper in days gone by, what was meant was the slightly écru tone that unbleached paper took on from the linen and the sheep's wool, the original material from which paper was made. Even today this tone is the most beautiful of all.

What catches the untrained eye in a collection of printing papers is of course the detergent-white offset paper, which was never meant to be used for books. It was to be used for color prints, which turn out more authentic when the paper background is stark white. For the same reason most art paper today is coated white on both sides. For years I have raised my voice, asking for art paper that is ever so slightly toned, but, alas, so far in vain. It would be highly desirable, but nobody stocks it.

Perhaps because the people in the offices of print shops fall victim to the allure that emanates from a sheet of stark white blank paper; perhaps also because some feel it's more ‹modern› – does it not remind one of refrigerators, modern sanitary appliances and the dentist's office? – or perhaps because white offset works best for art prints and no one makes toned art paper; because one wants the finished product to be ‹brilliant›; and perhaps also because inexperienced lay persons had a say in the matter, we have so terribly many pure white books today. Even the covers of books here and there are beginning to show up in the white garment of innocence. I am digressing, but white book covers are an expression of the same unhealthy tendency, and extremely delicate to boot.

The men responsible for these books, do they ever read their own products? Since they know them, perhaps they don't waste more than a glance. But proper reading is quite a different thing. Presumably they read books other than those they themselves have made and notice there how painful a stark white page can be. Not only is it cold and unfriendly, it is also upsetting because, like snow, it blinds the eye. Instead of blending with the type area and becoming one unit, the white hue of the paper retreats into a different optical plane, which creates an unpleasant effect of transparency.

By itself, to misuse white offset paper for book printing is already a sign of careless production. The detrimental effect of a white page is further reinforced by the desolate bleakness of the paper surface, which lacks almost all texture. Most fonts in use today are overly smooth and regular anyway, a fact especially evident in machine typesetting. All this combined creates an impression of extreme smoothness and cold, a kind of mirror of the indifference that at times prevails when books are made. But a good-looking book must not ever be the result of ingenious calculations and minimal expenditure of energy alone. If we frequently garner foreign praise for our books, this has to be a tribute paid our highly developed printing technique rather than the intrinsic beauty

of our books.* Many nations do not have these means of production, yet disregard for the book as an object in its own
right is just as widespread there as it is here. If the book is a
necessity then one has to overlook any technical deficiencies,
of course. High sales figures for a scientific work do not imply that the book itself is beautifully made. Doing no more
than what is absolutely necessary does not amount to art. Art
begins with the seemingly superfluous. Only when a book
presents itself so pleasantly, when the object *book* is so perfect that we would spontaneously like to buy it and take it
home, only then might it be a genuine example of the art of
making books.

Good-looking paper contributes no less to the overall at-
tractiveness of a book than does cultivated typography. This
is often overlooked. How extremely rare are books whose
paper betrays the hand of a knowledgeable and learned paper
designer! For one can design the paper precisely for the book
at hand. One can consider the relationship between thickness
and flexibility, the character of the font used, the mood of the
book, and then specify paper texture, hue and weight so as to
achieve perfect harmony among all parts. Our paper mills are
quite capable and prepared to grant such wishes. And it need
not even be more expensive.

In any case, it is desirable that stark white paper be used
only where absolutely required by the work on hand. And I
find it difficult to imagine such a case. If the phrase ‹petal
white› is used as a recommendation for paper, it constitutes
a deplorable abuse of our enjoyment of flowers. White petals
are beautiful indeed, but their color is not a suitable nuance
for the pages of a book. The term ‹snow white› paper is used

---

* *This and the following sentence refer to Switzerland.* – J T

171

less frequently, perhaps because deep down a feeling for the correctness of things still remains.

During and after years of national poverty, much grey and musty-yellow paper can be found in books. When the hard times are over, people rightly expect their books once again to be made from beautiful and durable paper. But the lay person is mistaken in his opinion that good paper has to be pure white and tinted paper is not durable. The expert should know that this is a fallacy. He should explain. We have pure white paper that yellows within ten years, just as there is distinctly grey paper of the finest quality!

Whiteness is never a sure sign of quality and durability. Lightly tinted book printing paper – the tint as a rule almost unnoticeable – is superior. It doesn't blind the eye and it promotes a harmony between paper and print that can be achieved on white paper only in rare and exceptional cases.

To reiterate, the whiteness of a paper says nothing about its durability. Because it dazzles the eye, it is unsuitable for printing books. What is necessary is a delicate toning toward écru or chamois. Even quite inexpensive books and magazines, and newspapers as well, should be printed on tinted paper rather than on pure grey.

Besides, certain scripts simply demand papers of definite tone and texture. This is especially true of the new cuts of classical type. The older the script, the darker and rougher the paper has to be. In fact, the Poliphilus roman (1499) on white paper has none of its rightful authority. It is brought out only on paper which in tone and character resembles that of the time around 1500. The same goes for Garamond roman (around 1530). In the latter part of the eighteenth century, a preference for ‹white› paper developed, and this is why Baskerville roman (around 1750) and Walbaum roman (around 1800) work best with paper that is nearly white (luckily, the bleaching process at the time wasn't nearly as perfect as it is today). The Bodoni roman alone (around 1700), in large sizes and on large pages only, can stand ‹stark white› paper – provided, however, it has a certain surface texture. This is because Bodoni deliberately cultivated the extreme contrast between the agitated black-and-white type on the one hand, and the white, fairly smooth paper on the other – an effect, by the way, that makes pleasant reading difficult. And the nineteenth century followed in his footsteps. The musty-yellow paper Bodoni used during the last decades of his life was less a matter of choice than a consequence of carelessly letting paper manufacture deteriorate. Today, most of his paper looks unsightly.

Toning of papers today is achieved by adding color pigments. Countless variations are possible when altering color, composition, sizing, and in particular surface texture. We should not forget this, and should make use of it as often as possible.

Ten Common Mistakes
in the Production of Books

1. *Deviant formats:* Books that are needlessly large, needlessly wide and needlessly heavy. Books have to be handy. Books wider than the ratio 3:4 (quarto), especially square ones, are ugly and impractical; the most important good proportions for books were and are 2:3, Golden Section and 3:4. The hybrid format A5 is particularly bad, while the hybrid format A4 is at times not entirely unsuitable. The inner book, or book block, of books that are too wide – square books in particular – will drop at the face. It is not easy to shelve or otherwise store books that are wider than 25 cm; 9⅞ in.

2. *Inarticulate and shapeless typesetting* as a consequence of suppressing indents. Unfortunately, this bad habit is encouraged by business schools, who teach, quite erroneously, that writing letters without indents is ‹modern›. One should not believe that this is merely ‹a matter of taste›. Here readers and nonreaders separate.

3. *Opening pages without any initial,* pages that begin bluntly in the upper left-hand corner and look like any other random page of text. One thinks he is seeing something other than a beginning. The opening of a chapter must be marked by a wide blank space above the initial line, by an initial letter or by something distinctive.

4. *Lack of form,* a consequence of the stillness of using only one size of type. It is difficult for any reader to find his

way around in a book where chapter openings are not accentuated and where title and imprint have been set in lowercase only in the size of the basic font.

5. *White, and even stark white, paper.* Highly unpleasant for the eyes and an offense against the health of the population. Slight toning (ivory and darker, but never crème), never obtrusive, is usually best.

6. *White book covers.* Equally confounding. They're about as delicate as a white suit.

7. *Flat spines on bound books.* The spines of bound books must be gently rounded; if they're not, the book will be cockeyed after reading, and the middle signatures will protrude.

8. *Gigantic vertical lettering on spines* that are wide enough to carry a horizontal inscription. Titles on the spine need not be legible from far away.

9. *No lettering on the spine at all.* Inexcusable for books more than 3 mm thick. How does one relocate such a booklet? The author's name must not be missing. It often determines the position of a book on the shelf.

10. *Ignorance of or disregard for the correct use of small caps, cursive and quotation marks:* see page 11 of.

Index

FORM OF THE BOOK *has been typeset by The Typeworks of Pt. Roberts, Washington, in Linotype Sabon, a face designed by Jan Tschichold in the early 1960's and released in 1964. The text of the book was designed by Vic Marks in close adherence to Jan Tschichold's principles of book design. It has been printed and bound by Thomson-Shore, Inc. of Dexter, Michigan. The paper is Glatfelter Offset Laid.*